When I think of Vicky, I am remir sayings from John Wimber, one of the Vineyard movement: "Nev a limp." More than just a phys..... .... statement underscores that all leaders who persevere have faced fiery trials and setbacks in their lives and ministry. This sums up Vickie's life and journey. Her riveting story is a testimony of how to respond to adversity and setback. A testimony of how we respond when we don't know or understand God's will at times in His plan for our lives. Yet, it is not just a story of surviving and overcoming a life-threatening disease. It also is a story of moving from an understanding of conditional love to unconditional love. Her given name – Victoria – beautifully describes her destiny and her walk with Jesus. Facing initial diagnosis of amputation and possible death from this disease, Vicky outlines how many areas of her life were amputated, enabling her the opportunity to see what was really important in her life: her faith in an unfailing God, despite the circumstances, her family and her community. This story is honest and unflinching; just like so many Biblical stories of people like us who had to wander through wilderness seasons only to come out on the other side stronger and wiser and having a deeper sense of God's grace and steadfastness. People like Jacob, who wrestled the angel, are never the same. He limps, yet is forever changed after his encounter with the living God. I'm so grateful that Victoria chose to share her, Paul's and her family's story with us.

Nicky Cruz
Evangelist and Author

My friend Vicky Lloyd is the real deal, and this book is gutsy and inspirational. I know that it will be a help to so many who face life's massive challenges.
**Andy Hawthorne OBE Founder & CEO,
The Message Trust**

Having lost my mum and several friends to cancer, this book really caught my attention. It's really possible to beat this terrible disease. This is a true story and one I have witnessed first-hand as a friend and co-labourer of the author in the City of Manchester. Her life is threatened and she fights back with everything she has. Read this book and learn from her faith.
Debra Green OBE Founder of Redeeming Our Communities

I have known Paul and Vicky Lloyd and have been impacted by their ministry for well over a decade. I clearly remember them going through this difficult season. What a journey! I found this book really inspiring, challenging and captivating. It gives an inside look on how faith works whilst in the mist of trials. It's raw, it's honest and it's faith-building. I believe this book will provide encouragement and tools for many people navigating through the various challenges we face in life.
James Aladiran, Founder, Prayer Storm

My friend Vicky Lloyd is the real deal! Her story will make you gasp and also celebrate. Read and be inspired that you can survive and thrive through whatever life throws at you.
Matt Bird, CEO of NAYBA

Through her personal journey of battling cancer, Vicky shares a story of resilience, determination and miraculous healing. This is a deeply inspiring and faith-building book that will leave readers feeling uplifted and encouraged. Vicky's unwavering faith in God and her positive attitude in the face of adversity is truly inspiring and serves as an example to us all. I highly recommend this book to anyone looking for inspiration and hope in the face of life's challenges. It's a beautiful tribute of faith and belief in the miracle-working power of God.

Georgina Valdez, Multi-regional Leader and senior pastor's wife of Victory Outreach Church in San Diego

Vicky's journey is a testimony of how God can use the medical profession, the prayers and faith of God's people; but, most importantly, that gritty in-your-face kind of faith and the determination of a young woman who wouldn't allow cancer to have the final say! I'm privileged to know and honoured to be a friend of Vicky and her family and to have witnessed what God can do.

**Mitchel Peterson, Pastor and Elder,
Victory Outreach International**

I am delighted that Vicky is getting this vital part of her Christian walk of faith into a book. As I have been blown away by her faith in God over 22 years, you will also be inspired as you read this amazing truth about triumph and belief in the healing power of Jesus Christ. Well done my friend. It was an honour and privilege to walk alongside you.

**Fiona Myles, adoption champion,
Mentor and Author.**

It never ceases to amaze me how God uses the foolish things of the world to confound the wise. He uses them to be a trophy and witness of what God can do. Vicky is definitely a treasure out of darkness! I have had the pleasure and honour to have seen her at the start of her walk with God and have been there along her journey of faith. To see her growth and development is truly a joy. I have always felt that God would use Vicki's life to impact many others. Continue to tell your story Vicki, and may God bless you and all that you put your hands to. Personally, I am so proud of you, your accomplishments and even more proud to call you my friend!
**Nellie Peterson Elder and Pastor's wife,
Victory Outreach International**

*Vicky shares her personal journey through bone cancer with honesty and vulnerability, recounting the challenges she faced as she navigated the medical system, underwent treatment and coped with the emotional and physical toll of the disease.
She reflects on the broader implications of her experience, including how her upbringing and faith shaped her approach to life. She offers valuable insights into the human experience of illness and recovery, highlighting the impact on loved ones and the wider community. This powerful and relatable book is a testament to the resilience of the human spirit, inspiring readers to find hope and strength in the face of adversity.*
**Tarnya Coley, award-winning Publisher,
Author and international speaker**

"

Through the pages of Cancer vs. the Bionic Me, Vicky Lloyd takes us on a real and raw journey through her battle with cancer and her incredible triumph over unimaginable odds. Her story of resilience reminds us all that even in the face of life's darkest moments; there is light. She is a modern-day miracle and is a great testimony of God's miracle-working power. Her unimaginable pain had a greater purpose than she could have imagined. Ephesians 3:20 says it best, "Now to him who is able to do immeasurably more than all we ask or imagine, according to his power that is at work within us." This is a must-read for anyone seeking inspiration and the belief that anything is possible. Prepare to be moved, inspired, and forever changed by this amazing story."

Doreen Cotinola, Victory Outreach International United Women in Ministry Overseer & Pastors Wife of Victory Outreach Whittier

CANCER
vs the
BIONIC ME

One Woman's struggle for survival.

Dedication

This book is dedicated, firstly to my saviour and
Lord Jesus Christ, and secondly to my family.
My amazing husband, Paul and Lilie, Tomas
and my beautiful mum, who all
mean the world to me.

Thanks

Last, but not least, I want to thank the ministry of
Victory Outreach International who have given
me purpose and opportunities to walk out
my salvation with joy.

Contents

Foreword

As a pastor's wife for more than fifty-five years, I've seen many people who have experienced healing through treatment. In this book, Vicky Lloyd shares a different kind of healing – a healing that can only be attributed to the power of God. Vicky shares her own journey of both physical and spiritual healing, and how she came to know God in a deeper way through this experience. This book is a reminder that there is more to healing than just physical restoration and that God can use our struggles to draw us closer to Him.

I am thrilled to introduce this book, because I know Vicky personally and have prayed with her through her struggles and subsequent miraculous healing. I believe this book will be an encouragement to all who read it.

Julie Arguinzoni
Co-founder of Victory Outreach International

Introduction

It could be said that I am a survivor. It's true that I've managed to get through some situations in my life that should have taken me out. Some of those experiences were the self-inflicted consequences of bad decisions, but others were things that people everywhere struggle to make any sense of. The biggest of my challenges was cancer. To be precise, my personal fight was with something called Parosteal Osteosarcoma, which is more commonly understood as a very rare form of bone cancer. That battle nearly ended my life. It definitely changed my life forever. I survived – I am grateful for that. But I don't just want to be remembered as having survived; I want to be remembered for how I have thrived.

Cancer was my enemy, and its effects are now my reality. The journey that could have just been a tale of fear and pain and horror – and it was all that – actually became an adventure of forgiveness, faith and friendship. It's been hard-going and long, but I'm still here. My life is different now in so many ways: I'm officially disabled but only physically. In many other ways, I've become freer than I ever was before my diagnosis.

There are many lessons I've learned as I travelled the path and I hope I can help others who have been forced to walk a similar one. It's for that reason, I finally sat down to write.

This book is not for everyone: it's real and it's raw. It's not the path I would've chosen, but it's the path I found myself on. The book looks at the decisions I had to make when things didn't go the way I'd planned. This book is a journey of my diagnosis and the ups and downs I faced and how I faced them. I didn't know what the outcome would be but I knew I had to make decisions about how I was going to respond to what was happening. It wasn't easy and there were days I really didn't think I was going to make it – not just physically but also mentally and emotionally. Our battles are not just physical ones, our souls and spirit play an important part as well.

What do I believe anyway?

Before we get going, we need to look at our concepts of life. Concepts are defined by dictionaries as something conceived in the mind; abstract ideas. We all have a belief system that comes from our grid of experience taken from our upbringing and the things that have happened to us that have coloured the way we see the world. Our concepts are more important than we often recognise because when there's something wrong with them, we end up living with misconceptions that can limit our reality.

My concept of life began with (what could be seen as) a middle class upbringing. My parents were in the RAF when I was born, which had us moving to different places to live. After they finished their service and entered civilian life, my dad worked really hard to support us and my mum made our house a home. I was born in 1971 and I have an older brother.

Looking back, even though it looked as if we had quite an ordinary life on the surface, there were a few dynamics that began to influence my belief system. Maybe because of his military background, Dad was strict and distant and there were a lot of expectations. In our house, if you didn't do well, the feeling my brother and I had was like we'd failed somehow. I've come to realise now that this is called conditional love. Growing up with that view of love really framed how I saw the world with its overriding attitude: I'll do this for you if I get what I want, or expect, in return.

I didn't realise it at the time but my belief system became transactional with fear, control, blame and punishment embedded in the fabric of who I was. This caused me to think that it's always someone's fault when things happen, which led to a mindset that somebody always needs to pay or be punished. Keep that in mind as we move through this story of my diagnosis of cancer.

Today, I'm a Christian, but I wasn't always a believer and I wasn't raised in a home that had God in it. My mum was adopted at birth in Northern Ireland and the person who took her and became my grandmother – an amazing woman who we called Granbea – was the only one who took my brother and I to church when we were young. I remember it as a good experience but it wasn't a regular thing; and the fact is that regardless of what anyone believes, when one has a diagnosis of cancer, we are all faced with the same mortality questions. Whatever beliefs you have, they will be tested.

The words "you have a twenty-three-centimetre tumour in your left leg, and the only prognosis is amputation," will definitely do something to you. For me the whole room seemed to shrink and the consultant's voice slowed down and the thoughts came to mind: Am I going to die? Where will I go if I die?

Whatever your focus is before hearing the words "you've got cancer," it becomes insignificant and life narrows all the way down to what's important. My family became very important and in surprising ways. My faith became very important. My concepts of how both of those things worked were jumbled up and rearranged in the most amazing ways, and that has forever altered the way I view life. I thank God now for that, but I didn't thank Him on that day.

On that terrible day when I received my diagnosis of cancer, I had gone to the hospital alone. I had already been there in the previous weeks for some scans and tests. Then it seemed as if they were steering towards an opinion that what I had been feeling in my leg was not cancerous. A biopsy was taken to be sure and I'd come in for the results, not expecting any bad news. I was confident that everything would be the same as before, so my husband, Paul, was with our two young children doing the necessary school stuff.

Lilie was six at the time and Tomas was three. I remember calling Paul and just blurting out what the doctor had told me in that room. It stuck in my mind that it all seemed to be so matter of fact to the doctors that they wanted to cut off my leg. It was shocking and horrifying to me. It's my leg! Paul was calm on the phone—that's him all over – but I was losing it. In fact, everything is pretty much a blur from then on as I entered my survival zone. It was a zone I'd stay in for eight years as I fought for my life. I'm on the other side of that long, dark valley now. This is my story.

Chapter 1
You Have Cancer!

I have to take you back to the day when my whole world seemed to tilt to one side and my thoughts were that this must be happening to someone else. I had been having pain in my left leg for a little over three years. I had attended many doctor's appointments and had all sorts of scans, but it was never considered that there could be anything to really worry about. But that day completely blindsided me. It was almost a knockout blow and it left me reeling.

But before that, it is probably best to rewind a little bit, so that there's a bit more context to what led up to this – because there's a mad backstory.

When my son, Tomas, was two days old, I had fallen down the steep stairs in the Edwardian terrace house that we were living in. I was exhausted, as any mother would be with a toddler of two and a newborn baby. The stairs were steep – Mount Everest steep – and I remember being half-way down with Tomas in my arms when I fell.

All I could think of was not to fall on Tomas. Somehow I managed some mummy gymnastics, and by instinct put out my left leg to manoeuvre myself around. I still went down and the weight of my body was concentrated on my leg. But my baby was safe. I remember feeling such pain that I thought I was going to pass out, but all I could think about was Tomas. I looked at his little perfect head and those trusting eyes looking up at me and the pain didn't matter! Hey, I had just given birth and compared to that pain, this was nothing! That's where I think it all started.

From that day on, I had pain in my left leg and a lump developed on the side of it, but I just left it to heal. If I'm honest, I didn't really think much of it. I know that might sound a little crazy, but in comparison to how I was feeling at that time, it didn't matter.

The reality was, I had the beginnings of postnatal depression. It's a very scary thing when there's nothing you can do to change the sense of hopelessness you're feeling at what should be the happiest time of your life. I'd just given birth to a beautiful son and yet everything felt so dark inside me. Anyone out there who has been through this will know it's so frightening and strange that you're scared to even put words to it.

I think the realisation that I was suffering with this horrible condition only became clear when I watched a story on the evening news. A woman with newborn twins had walked out of her home, left her children and committed suicide because of postnatal depression. I understood those feelings! I could sense the depths of darkness that that poor mum must have been experiencing.

I must add here that I'm a woman of faith who believes in and has followed Jesus since my first experience with Him in 2000. Sometimes, I think having faith can be confused with never going through dark times by some people, but the Bible is full of people going through valleys and dark times and even depression. What a wake-up call that was for me! Looking back now, I'm sure that's the reason why my leg pain was not at the forefront of my mind. It took me at least six months to come through that dark and lonely time, and my mind was in shadow for a lot longer than that. If anyone reading this has had similar thoughts, please speak to someone about what you're going through. Help is available.

It was only when the dark clouds began to lift that I was in the right headspace to see my GP about the discomfort in my leg. He immediately referred me to the orthopaedic department at Trafford Hospital, and after examining it, he proceeded to tell me that I had actually fractured my leg when I had fallen down the stairs with Tomas and that it had healed a bit crookedly all on its own! The doctor looked at me as if to say, "How did you not realise you'd broken your leg?" I think I just mumbled some confusing stuff about having a newborn baby and dark thoughts and falling down stairs. It must've sounded so crazy.

The doctor gave me the option to have surgery to straighten my leg, which I agreed to. That operation went well, and they shaved some bone from my tibia and straightened the crooked part of the bone. I ended up with my first scar. Little did I know it would be the first of many more to come.

A year passed and I'd been having some pain in the same leg that had been operated on. It got to the point that I could hardly walk. The only way I could describe it is that it felt like something was growing inside. I went back to my GP and he said it was probably inflammation of the muscle. It continued to get worse. I went back again and pushed them until I was eventually referred back to the surgeon in Trafford who had performed the original surgery.

This consultant sent me for a scan and he called me back a week later. I remember walking into his office and he had the scan in front of him on the screen. I remember that day as everything went into slow-motion. He had his legs crossed and his arms folded and said the strangest thing: "Mrs Lloyd, from this point on, I'm not able to discuss the results with you any further. We've found a mass on your left leg and I am going to refer you to a tumour specialist at The Christie Hospital in Manchester."

He picked up the phone and called someone, who I presume had already seen the scan results. Looking intently at me, he said, "Can you make your way to Christie's hospital now?"

A mass? Tumour specialist? What on earth was he talking about?

I told him that I understood that it was inflammation of the muscle as a result of the fall in which I had fractured my leg and he had already operated on it to repair the fracture. That's what he'd said all along. How had this turned into a tumour all of a sudden? He was very quiet, and asked, "Can you go there now?"

It all felt a bit surreal: I remember walking out of the hospital and getting into my old, blue Ford Focus to drive to the other hospital – the cancer hospital! I was on my own because my husband, Paul, was with our two very young children, Lilie and Tomas. After all, we thought it was just going to be a routine appointment.

In that moment, the world felt and looked different: it felt like it went a different shade – a bit darker – and I had an awareness that something could be very wrong. I quickly tried to adjust myself. They must have it wrong, it's a mistake. Let me just go home and ignore it. Isn't it amazing what the mind does to cope?

I called Paul and relayed what had been said. I then drove to the Christie Hospital and sat in another office to be told I was being referred to a bone cancer specialist at a hospital at Oswestry, on the border with Wales. "Would I be available to go there in the next few days as it would take some time to send my scans over?"

And that's where my cancer journey began!

From a silly fall to pain in my leg, to being sent from one place to another with the experts changing their minds from one diagnosis to another. Imagine being told it's one thing, even having surgery for it, to then being told they hadn't seen this dangerous mass when they operated on me. Now I've possibly got some kind of tumour!

The appointment was arranged within the next couple of days, and this time I went with Paul to meet the consultant at the Robert Jones and Agnes Hunt Orthopaedic Hospital. He told me that it may not be cancer after all, and they would need to do a biopsy to determine what was happening in my leg. It's funny how we grab hold of the slightest bit of hope that comes our way, isn't it?

I left Oswestry telling myself that everything was OK. They gave me a date for the biopsy and it was to be done just before Paul and I travelled to Los Angeles to attend a conference, where Paul would be one of the keynote speakers. I was told that it would take about ten days for the results to come back, which meant we'd receive them around the time we returned.

We flew to LA, and I can remember that the conference was being held at the Los Angeles Convention Center, located in the Downtown area. Our hotel was about three blocks away and we thought we would be able to take a gentle stroll there every day for the sessions. It was the World Conference for the Church movement we're part of called Victory Outreach International.

Paul and I had been pastoring the Victory Outreach Manchester church for almost eight years at this time, seeing it grow from a handful of people to several hundred. It was exciting that Paul would be speaking to almost twenty thousand people from all over the world. While we were there, Paul's parents would look after our children for the very first time.

What should have been a spiritual mountain-top experience with friends whilst experiencing the delights of a new city was overshadowed by intense pain in my leg. It was affecting my ability to walk and sleep; I was glad when it was time to come home.

I remember landing in Manchester and receiving a phone call from the hospital while we were in the car on the way home from the airport.

"Can you come to the hospital as soon as possible?"

I looked at Paul and felt my stomach lurch. We made arrangements once more for our children to be taken care of, and we drove the sixty miles to the hospital the next day. I felt like I was on a roller coaster of emotions.

The results were back from the biopsy. It was low grade cancer, which had turned at the bottom of the tumour to high grade. That's when they gave me the news that would shape the rest of my life.

"You have a twenty-three-centimetre tumour in your left leg. We believe it's something called Parosteal Osteosarcoma, which is one of the rarest forms of bone cancer around and is usually found in children and is only seen in about one per cent of the UK population."

The consultant then went on to say something that I struggled to even begin to receive and which would cast it's shadow in my mind for the next ten years.

"I am very sorry, Mrs Lloyd. The tumour is very large and the only thing we can do for you, is to remove your leg from the thigh down. With this type of bone cancer, chemotherapy has a very low success rate and the best form of treatment is limb removal."

I remember looking at the consultant's mouth moving and hearing the words, but it didn't compute. Who was he talking about? What was he talking about? We'd gone from possible cancer to not having cancer, to now having it and the only thing they could do for me was to cut off my leg. It didn't feel real.

I remember asking this one question: "Where would they do this amputation?" He replied that an amputation is very simple and quick, and any hospital can do it. He said it in such a matter of fact way!

Everything within me screamed, "NO! What do you means it's very simple and very quick? NO! You're talking about me here, I am a person and not a hospital number. You're talking about my leg. It shouldn't be just a simple and easy thing!"

The consultant carried on, "Mrs Lloyd, you are young [I was 39 years old at the time] and you have the chance to be healthy. You have two young children. We have to remove it otherwise this type of cancer spreads to the lungs and it can kill you. The best thing we can do to remove the tumour is to remove your leg. It's too big to do anything else."

I was taken into a yellow room and sat opposite a nice lady who smiled and looked at me with a sad but kind face. "I know it's a lot to take in," she said as she handed me leaflets on cancer and support. I had to go away and make a decision about when the amputation should happen. I just felt numb. It felt like I was having an out of body experience, looking in on someone else's life. But it was happening to me.

We drove home in silence, speechless about what we had just heard. I remember looking at Paul and saying, "What am I going to do? Why is this happening to me?" There were so many questions, but no immediate answers.

As we drove back to our little terraced house and our children, everything around me looked normal – but my life had changed irreversibly in the last few hours.

How could this happen to me? What was I going to do?

Chapter 2
Is There Anybody Out There?
Is God Real Enough?

Is God real? Well, there's a question!

For most of my life I didn't really believe in God, possibly due, in part, to my dad's unbelief. But through choices I made in my teenage years, I was faced with some challenges that led me to exploring whether God was real.

I wasn't looking for God, but I came to the understanding that He was looking for me. I asked this seemingly abstract God into my life when I was twenty-seven years old and had an experience that changed me forever. I had said to this God, who I wasn't sure I believed in, that He would need to show me He was real and take away the addiction that had held me captive for ten years (but that's another book).

Long story short: just like my experience with cancer, the moment I prayed to a God I hadn't known before and put my trust in Him, it changed me forever. It was like someone came and changed the lens I was looking at life through (a bit like an optician when you're having an eye test done). Suddenly, the way I saw the world changed and it seemed as if there was more colour. I saw things in a different shade: I could smell living things, I could see clearly and the desire to take drugs left me.

For those of you reading this who want to switch off right now, please don't. This isn't a book solely about God, but about my journey with cancer, of which God played a massive part. I cannot erase God from this journey because He was so present throughout all of it. This once abstract God came and did something so personal and real to me that it really got my attention.

My issues hadn't just come from an addiction to drugs, but all the things that lay beneath the drugs. The drugs, at first, covered my personal pain and darkness, but eventually they took me deeper and deeper into more pain and darkness. Now, at twenty seven, that darkness was penetrated and God did something no one else could. I have no doubt in my mind that my addiction was broken because of Him. I understand that there are people who stop taking drugs without God and they can stay clean without faith in the Him. However, my life has been empowered and guided by my faith in the Creator God.

In my experience, there's something so deep and personal that has taken place in me that I can't deny God's reality. My husband wrote his MA dissertation about how the gospel brings transformation to people with lived experiences of addiction. He's personally seen hundreds and hundreds of men and women freed from addiction after engaging with God. Add to that how many of these treasures out of darkness we've come across in our ministry worldwide and it would be in the tens of thousands, from up to forty different nations. My husband has written about the fact that everyone is broken somewhere (either externally, internally or eternally) and how God can fix those areas and transform people; not just reform them. We've known people with PhDs connect with God and seen politicians and professional footballers being transformed, so it's not just about the poor junkies that are desperate for something to help them. My experiences, for all the years since my own first encounter with Jesus, have cemented my belief in His reality and power and love.

Here's where things get interesting, though. You think you know what you believe until something comes along to really test that belief. Cancer did that for me. When I was diagnosed, I'd been a Christian for a little over a decade and had seen some amazing things happen around me. It wasn't just a nice, safe little cultural church bubble that I was involved in; it was raw and real and full of interesting people from some pretty wild backgrounds.

The ministry I was part of then (and still am as I write this book), Victory Outreach International, is an inner city ministry that concentrates on people on the margins of society. Backgrounds of heavy addiction and crime are common but, surprisingly, mixed with students, doctors and nurses; business owners and academics; young and old. What should, in all honesty, be an explosive blend of cultures with no right to mix together, becomes an environment for transformation as each person adds something unique and life-giving to their neighbour.

I believed I'd seen enough of God to never be shaken, but I was wrong. I've come to understand that you can't do anything to prevent being shaken – it's outside your control. All you can do is to hope that your roots and foundations go deep enough to keep you standing when things stop shaking.

Did I believe in divine healing? Did I believe in miracles? Yes, I did. But when I heard those words, "You've got cancer," the big question I had, rather became, "Was God going to heal me?" Suddenly, it became very personal.

Then came the torrent of questions: Do I have enough faith? Why has this happened to me? Was I being punished for something? How am I going to deal with this? I even had to deal with the thought that, because I was serving God, I really didn't deserve to get sick!

Why me? Was I being punished for all those years I'd been living a crazy lifestyle? Was it some kind of payback? Was I involved in some type of sin that I was unaware of? I checked myself deeply. I read the Scriptures and examined my life. In all honesty, I was so confused by it all. Please understand, all this was happening quickly: I'm talking hours and days and sleepless nights.

This is the reality that often gets covered over by religious talk and the subtle pride that we all struggle with. I really want to be honest with you, though, and if you're coming with me on this journey, be prepared for some exposure and vulnerability.

Sadly, I've come across many people – even in churches – that stay sick because they couldn't bring themselves to admit they weren't well or admit they had doubts and fears. The truth is that there's no solution to a wrongly diagnosed problem or a hidden and secret one or one to which you won't admit. The best thing is to always be as honest as you can be. I was scared, angry and confused and in a state of shock. Anyone who's ever felt that and been in that kind of turmoil will know that making decisions is really difficult. What I needed was an anchor point, something to pin my hopes on. My mind latched onto a situation I'd faced about ten years previously.

When I first became a Christian, my liver was messed up. It was my own doing as I had abused it mercilessly through my years of crack, heroin and alcohol use. I'd been diagnosed with hepatitis B and the diagnosis furthermore concluded that I had cirrhosis. At that time, I felt very unwell and it was painful. I was also bright orange! I can laugh now because I'm on the other side of it. But I was really sick and the medical specialists tried me on a new-to-market medication that would supposedly stimulate antibodies within my body to fight the hepatitis.

I was one of the first people to be given a new tablet form of Interferon. The thinking was that if it worked, I wouldn't have to have a liver transplant. The challenge was that there were a lot of side effects. I constantly felt extremely tired with flu like symptoms and had low moods. My weight ballooned and my life was pretty grim. Actually, it was a horrible time and not something I'd ordinarily be looking back to.

At the time, I was new in my faith – I'd only been a Christian for a little over a year. Therefore, I didn't really understand how the whole divine healing thing worked. But I'd been so touched by the person of Jesus, I knew He could do something. Maybe, I wondered, He could even add something to what the doctors were trying to do.

I'd been on the liver medication for a year and remember that after being in bed for a few days, I found myself crawling to the hospital and speaking to my consultant about how horrible I was feeling all the time. I was supposed to be on the medication for five years, but I couldn't do it anymore. I told him I was taking myself off the treatment. He told me I was mad and that I needed this medication, he said to me, "You are a very sick women." This wasn't the first time that I'd been told that for many different reasons – and not all of them were physical. Nevertheless, I stopped taking the medication that day having decided to trust God to help me figure things out. My consultant asked me to go back monthly to have scans and blood tests so that the team could monitor me. I agreed to do this.

Then came the moment and this would be my anchor point! Sometime after I had stopped the treatment earlier than the doctors recommended, I'd been for a scan at The Royal Free Hospital in London. They'd taken all the usual blood tests and I sat in the consultant's office with Paul, waiting for the results.

My doctor was behind his computer and he looked puzzled. He lifted his eyes to me and said, "Mrs Lloyd, something very strange has happened. I've never seen this before. Your body has started to build its own antibodies to fight the HepB. I don't actually think this is possible after a year of medication so I want to continue to monitor this. Your liver looks very healthy."

You'll never know how amazing that news was to me. From being far too close to needing a liver transplant, to hearing that my liver looked very healthy was a turnaround that nobody expected. But I'd really believed that God could do something special. I needed Him to help me and I think He did. What happened to my body wasn't natural and I believe there'd been divine intervention. I also started to realise that God can even work in conjunction with medicine. I've never understood the way some people think that believing in God makes you anti-science. That idea may be found on the extremes of the faith spectrum, but the same element of fanaticism can be found in those with an exclusively materialistic worldview, too. Any extremes are usually unhealthy. In my case, the medical intervention had definitely helped, but because the side effects were so intolerable, I couldn't continue with it. That should have meant my recovery was over. It's at the very end of our human capability where God reveals His ability.

I continued to go to the clinic for monitoring, but month after month the results were clear: My body was building its own antibodies, which shouldn't have happened and my liver had started to heal. I was told my liver was like that of a teenager! I was healthy and healed and able to continue with my life. This caused my faith to rocket. My colour had returned to normal and so had my weight. Life started looking good.

So, fast forward to 2011 and my cancer diagnosis. In the midst of the madness and turmoil, I'd found my anchor point. As far as healing was concerned, I really felt that God and I had this one down and that a twenty-three-centimetre tumour wasn't going to be a challenge for my God. Somehow, He would heal me because I not only believed He was real, but I also believed He still intervened in the world He created. Not only that, but He'd done it before for me and I had a special sense of His closeness to me, even in the middle of this new and horrible storm.

I knew it was going to be a massive battle, but I had a sense of peace knowing that I wouldn't have to fight it on my own. That's how faith works: it's not blind – like some people mockingly accuse it of being – it's based on evidence. When you look closely, and not just casually, you find evidence for God. As one famous writer once put it, it's like believing there's a sun. You might not always see it, but you can always see the evidence of what it does. That's how my faith in God works. I had that anchor point of evidence because He'd shown His hand before. The peace that gave me was going to be my refuge in the storms that would lash out at me over the next several years of my life.

Chapter 3
A Faith Crisis
What Happens Now?

I still had cancer. It hadn't shrunk or disappeared. Even though there were thousands of people praying for me all over the world, the diagnosis was the same. The only option I was given was limb removal, an amputation of my left leg above the knee.

So what do I do? Do I stand on God's Word and not have the operation? There were voices coming at me from all different angles, from people of faith and people of no faith. And let me be clear, there are some well-meaning nutters on both sides of the fence!

One Christian even said to me, "If you have the operation, you don't have enough faith!"

What needs to be said is there are some people who I think have a slightly warped view of what faith is. They place the emphasis on your act of believing, whilst not taking into account the object of your believing, the Creator God and His will and plan for the situation. You don't just work yourself up to a particular point where you feel like you're full of this thing called "faith" and then you launch it into whatever you're believing for.

Christian faith includes a hoping for something to happen, but then includes the evidence of a direction to take, based either on a previous biblical example; or a current sense of God leading you in a specific direction. This will be witnessed by clear circumstances and people around you often agreeing with what you're feeling. All of this is then activated by your obedience to do what you think God wants you to do. There's a lot of relational trust involved in the process of living a life of faith and maybe that's why some prefer a nice cut-and-dry religion, with a predictable and transactional god, over a living relationship with an interested and involved Saviour God. Then, there are those who either choose to ignore all that mad spiritual stuff, or actively oppose it.

I had no difficulty in believing that God was powerful enough to heal me instantly, but was that the plan? After all, I'd had treatment for hepatitis and God had used that and then taken it beyond what the experts thought could happen. When the hep consultant – who knew my faith – saw the results, it definitely opened his eyes to the possibility that something beyond his experience had actually happened in my case.

But I still had a battle raging inside me. My thoughts were shouting confused things, such as if I made a stand for my faith, then my God would miraculously heal me; but if I didn't, I'd be a failure. Then there was my previous experience to contend with: Why wasn't God moving in the same way He had before?

I kept expecting after each scan that I'd hear the words, "Mrs Lloyd, I can't believe what I am seeing, but the tumour has disappeared." But those words never came. Some might find that sad, or maybe have a little smile and think how foolish I was to believe that God is real and still does this stuff today. I assure you I've seen real miracles. My husband has also seen incredible things happen on his travels and in this book I'm trying to use personal examples that I have evidence for. My hepatitis experience was real and was definitely outside the boundaries of normality. Medical records that give all the information on what happened with that particular situation.

Regardless of all my previous experiences, however, and the faith I had in my God, nothing changed. We were told we had to make a decision about the amputation within one week. I say "we" because Paul was with me all the way. It's important to have someone with you in those rooms with the experts. Quite often, you'll be in some sort of shocked state, unable to grasp all that you're being told. When I couldn't think, Paul would ask the difficult questions and then he would translate it back to me when we were alone. So, I always fully understood what had been said. That helped me so much because nothing was making sense. It was not looking like a good outcome on any level. What should I do?

Paul's God encounter

What happened next will possibly sound a bit hard to believe, but it really happened. While we were in the horrible, stressful place of deciding what to do, Paul prayed and fasted. This is something we do when we need direction. Here's what happened in his words:

Paul: I'd just had a shower and was still in the bathroom. I'd been really praying about the situation with Vicky and I'd been asking the Lord why it was happening. I reminded Him that we were serving Him as faithfully as we could, we'd given up comfort and possessions and were doing our best to help people who had been in some dark places in life. So why was this happening to Vicky? I'll never forget what happened next. I clearly "heard" God's voice inside me. That's the only way I can describe it.

Clearly and strongly He said, "You must accept what I allow – but I will not allow them to take her leg."

It's very unusual for something like this to happen in this way, but I knew, without a doubt, that God had given me an instruction. I immediately went out and got Vicky and we sat down as I told her what had happened. No amputation! That was the clear message, but that was all we had to go on. The day of decision was fast approaching, but even though things were still not fully clear, I had a sense of complete peace all over me. I knew it was going to work out differently – and better – than everyone else thought.

The time came to go to see Mr Cool, the surgical consultant, with our decision. As we sat in his office there was a dark sense of foreboding. It was a foregone conclusion as far as they were concerned. As he asked Vicky what her decision was, I sensed God's presence again. Normally in these situations, it's only the patient who receives the attention of the doctors and whoever is with them is basically invisible.

Vicky looked at me and I opened my mouth and out came these words: "You're not going to do an amputation, you're going to do an extraction. You will get skills you've never learned. You will have favour you don't deserve. And this will be the one that will be written about in books."

Imagine the stunned expressions! I probably should have felt a bit stupid and embarrassed at blurting out such high-sounding nonsense, but I just felt an incredible sense of peace and certainty. Even Vicky was a bit stunned because we hadn't discussed this previously. I hadn't known I was going to say that before we went into that office, and I fully believe that God gave me those words. But after a few moments, Mr Cool looked at Vicky and said he'd have to take this decision to a multi-disciplinary team meeting for discussion and we'd hear from him in due course. We left the hospital in a state of...? I don't know, only that we were in a state. Within a day Vicky received a call from the hospital to come for another meeting.

So after another two-hour drive we were back in the same office. Mr Cool looked at Vicky and said, "The team has agreed to do an extraction and I will do the surgery."

Amazing! Unbelievable! What does that mean?

The consultant was very negative about the operation and went into worst case scenario doctor mode. He told Vicky there was only a small chance of it being successful and then when it all went bad, he'd still have to cut off her leg. They would give it their best shot but the tumour was so big he couldn't guarantee there would be safe enough margins; so there might still be some cancerous "seeds" left inside her. She was told that whatever happened, the movement of the leg would be limited and she would probably be in a wheelchair for the rest of her life.

Mr Cool described the operation to us and told Vicky in graphic detail what would happen. The leg would be opened up and the bones removed – tibia, fibula, knee –

and a silver coated titanium implant would be screwed into her femur, joined to a false kneecap, with the same artificial metal rod running down her leg and screwed into her ankle. A lot of muscle would be removed as well as most of her nerves. He told us that it would be by far the longest replacement ever done, and once again said that he didn't hold out much hope that it would be successful.

He mentioned that when he gave the measurements for the implant to the prosthetic technicians, they called and told him they thought he'd made a mistake in the size. He laughed when he said to us that he had told them, "That is the size!"

It all seemed so unreal. Then there was the cost of the procedure. Apparently, the implant would cost as much as a family car. I know it's wrong but I began telling Vicky that if she died before me, I wanted her leg so I could sell it for scrap and buy a car. Dark humour, I know, but humour is a definite antidote to doom and darkness in one of the worst times of our lives. Vicky laughs with me and that's what's important.

The ominous thing was when Vicky asked about the amputation cost she was told it wasn't really in the same league and that it could be done anywhere by any surgeon. There's a big difference, it seems, when you make a stand and fight for something, instead of just opting for the easy (for them) solution. Since then, I've told some of my friends whose spouses had contracted a serious illness, to listen well and fight for the best result, even when everything in you just wants to comply with the powers that be. I'm so glad we didn't agree to let them cut off Vicky's leg; and when you obey God, it all works out in the end.

Back to Vicky

I have to say that at this point, I heard everything that was being said and I knew that everyone was speaking about my life. But it felt like it was happening to someone else and I was just an observer. I called this chapter "A Faith Crisis" because I wanted the tumour to disappear and I wanted to be healed. I didn't really want an operation to remove most of the inside of my leg. I was in a crisis, even though I was a woman of faith.

I had to navigate in my mind what my life was going to look like and, if I'm honest, I was questioning where on earth God was in all of this. It almost felt like He'd left me. I wasn't some sort of spiritual giant – even though I was a Pastor's wife and co-leader of a thriving church – I was just a youngish women facing life-changing decisions in a time of massive pressure while trying to be a mum, a wife and just Vicky.

If you're in this kind of situation, have had a diagnosis, your world has been turned upside down with voices coming from everywhere, are searching the Scriptures on healing and wondering what you're supposed to do, then this book is just for you. I am right there with you; I've been there and spent years thrashing it all out.

I had to make a choice about amputation and I'd one week to do that. On top of all of this, I had two young children who relied on me. It was so horrible living in the reality of knowing I had cancer and also knowing that that thing inside my body could kill me at any time if I didn't do something about it.

One of the biggest challenges was that although I had pain in my leg, I felt really well in myself. I could have quite easily lived in denial and a lot of the time I had. Some of the hardest times I faced, were in the mornings. I think at that point you feel you are rested and your subconscious is at peace, but then, suddenly, my thoughts would go straight to the reality that I had cancer. A feeling of dread would come over me. I really couldn't see myself living without a leg. How would I cope with that?

I started going through all the questions I've already mentioned, plus what could be called recriminations. How had it grown to this size without anyone seeing it? What about the surgeon that operated on my fractured leg? Did he not see it? How was it missed? Someone was to blame for this! Surely the hospital got it wrong, or the doctors. I felt such a tension inside pulling me between the fact that I knew God was my Protector and wondering why He had not protected me from cancer. Where was He now – and why me?

I agreed to have the surgery and I'm so grateful to Paul for helping me negotiate this horrible decision. He was clear about what he believed God had shown him, but when all was said and done, it remained my choice alone.

The surgery was set for the 9 August 2011, my son, Tomas' fourth birthday. I remember the day before the operation: going out for a meal at the Trafford Centre with my family. It was so surreal as, again, I really had no idea what I was about to venture into. The next morning we travelled once again the two-hour journey from Manchester to Oswestry, on the border between England and Wales and I was taken in for all the pre-op stuff. They checked all my vital signs and then did something I'd struggle to get past for the next ten years: they drew an arrow on my left leg in marker pen! I kissed Paul and he walked with me as I was wheeled off towards the operating theatre. As I entered the elevator and the doors began to close, we looked at each other and waved – and then I was on my own.

My world was about to change...

Chapter 4
Gobbing In My Eyes
Strange Methods

One of the biggest truths I've found on my cancer journey is that there are different methods of healing – and not all of them happen in the way you thought, or hoped, they would.

This became my revelation as I moved from my faith crisis through the process of learning about the building blocks of faith that God wanted to use to get me through this horrible time. The first real building block in any type of transition is the place of acceptance.

I started to believe that God was going to heal me, but in a different way than I'd expected Him to. I had to come to a place of real understanding that He uses all things to work good in our lives, including medicine and surgeons and He was right in the midst of this story.

Before we continue, I have to comment a little on the title of this chapter. I know it's a random-sounding title, and if you're unfamiliar with the word "gobbing," it might be confusing. But I had to include it because of a story in the Bible that God used to speak to me about my personal situation. Firstly, the word "gobbing" is an English slang word for spitting and it was commonly used when I was growing up in the context of spitting aggressively at something. It didn't feel good to be "gobbed at" and many fights started because someone did that to a person who responded angrily. If I'm honest, that's what I felt had happened to me and I think one of the keys to this whole episode is about how you respond when something nasty like this happens to you. Let's look at the Biblical account before we move on:

John 9:1-3:

> *1 As Jesus was walking along, He saw a man who had been blind from birth. 2 "Rabbi," His disciples asked Him, "why was this man born blind? Was it because of his own sins or his parents' sins?"*
>
> *3 "It was not because of his sins or his parents' sins," Jesus answered. "This happened so the power of God could be seen in him."*

A major revelation I received through this story was that I didn't get cancer because I had personally sinned. Of course, I know we all sin as we come into contact with the brokenness of this world and its environments and systems and that we'll be contaminated with sickness, decay and eventually death. There are times that we will go through things that might have been brought about by wrong choices, bad diet and, yes, sin. But in some cases God wants to reveal His glory. I believe in my situation, and maybe even yours, that He wants to show something about Himself and how He accomplishes His purpose for our lives. Skip forward a few verses and we see what happens next:

John 9:6-7:

> *6 Then He spit on the ground, made mud with the saliva, and spread the mud over the blind man's eyes. 7 He told him, "Go wash yourself in the pool*

*of Siloam" (Siloam means "sent"). So the man went
and washed and came back seeing!*

This is the "gobbing" part I was talking about. Put yourself in his shoes for a moment. You can't see what's going on and then suddenly you're getting spat on! That's what it felt like for me when I was in a place of utter powerlessness and other people were imposing their stuff on me. Admittedly, I was probably in a state of shock at the time and really needed guidance with my decisions, but it still felt so invasive and uncomfortable. Something kicked in with me, however; something I'd been doing throughout my Christian walk. If it's God leading me, I'll obey and follow. Even though it must've been very strange to have someone make a paste out of dirt and spit and then rub it in his eyes, the blind man obeyed. His response wasn't defensive or angry but was humble and obedient. This spoke to me because I was about to embark on a step by step journey of obedience, which didn't make much sense to me.

In this account we see Jesus telling the man to, "Go wash yourself in the pool of Siloam" (Siloam means "sent"). As the man went and washed, something miraculous took place: he came back seeing! This bit is important and the whole account encouraged me at a time when I couldn't see a clear way forward. It felt like God had sent me in the direction I was going, though, and I sensed that my response to what I was going through would be crucial to the outcome I would see.

I don't profess to be a theologian – so don't jump on me – but the Word of God is alive and, I believe, applicable to us personally at different times. Therefore, reading and getting an understanding that it wasn't really this guy's fault that he was in the condition he was in and it wasn't because he had sinned, or his parents had sinned, really set me free. I think we can often trip out on the whole "punishment" idea, and when that mentality takes root it can push us away from the place of freedom into a deeper dungeon of self-recrimination and blame-shifting. The mindset that there was another possibility was really helpful to me.

On top of that, seeing this strange method that Jesus used to bring about the man's healing helped me to become reconciled to having this unusual surgical procedure that had been spoken about. I mean, spitting in the dirt and rubbing it in the poor man's eyes is not normal. And nor was the idea of God saving my life and bringing healing and restoration by having a stranger cut open my leg, remove the bones and the cancerous tumour and replacing everything with a massive silver-coated titanium implant! But I started to hope that it could work.

The biggest thing I was learning was how there are things that take place that aren't always as cut and dried as we think they should be. After all, God is God and He's ultimately in charge, so He can pretty much do things however He wants. If we're honest, we often have a problem with not being in control, which is one of the basic ingredients of what the Bible describes as "sin." It has dangerous consequences when we're tempted to do things our way and not God's way.

I sometimes wonder what might have happened if I'd just stayed in denial or listened to the "expert advice" of those who wanted to cut off my leg. I definitely think my life would've been either very much shorter or much more limited.

However, I received reassurance from God that every step of the way, I should simply trust Him and do what He wanted me to do. It was as if He was saying to me, "Vicky, trust this process I am taking you through. I know it doesn't make sense to you but I know the outcome. You haven't done anything wrong, but this is for the glory of God."

I have to admit, I still felt a little hurt at why it was me having to go through all this and why I needed to travel this path I was having to walk. These thoughts will come and they're normal. I ended up struggling with this for years but at that time I remembered reading biographies of people that had gone through tragic suffering as Christians and their response to it.

I especially remembered the story of Joni Eareckson Tada and the tragic accident that left her paralysed. What she went through, and the testimony of how God had met with her daily as she negotiated her way through the maze of emotions and decisions that faced her, became something I could anchor into. I took some small comfort that tragedy strikes other people too, but God guided her through a seemingly impossible situation and her story has given millions of people hope. I pray that my journey will bring hope in a similar way.

My cancer journey was a process using different methods of healing than those I would have chosen, but God was right there in the midst of my situation. His grace was enough and I received my daily bread, but the methods

He used often felt like He had "gobbed in my eyes." It's a strange tension to trust God and feel anger at what He was doing all at the same time. But, hey, if anyone was going to "gob" in my eyes, I'm glad it was my Creator, because He knew me before the foundations of the world had been established. And if He created my leg once, He could surely restore it.

I desperately wanted the power of God to be seen through my own personal situation, so if God wanted to use different methods, then that was fine. He never left me at any part of this process! In the next chapter, we will look at the different ways the Lord led me through using signposts, not footprints.

Chapter 5
Signposts Not Footprints
When the Lord Goes Before You

I believe that the Lord will always communicate with us, no matter what we go through and regardless of how hopeless it may seem. He wants us to know that He's our daily bread and that man cannot live on bread alone but on every word that comes out of His mouth to nourish us and sustain us. He does this in different ways, but I believe the main way He nourishes, sustains and communicates is through His Word, which anyone can read in the Bible.

Many people have opinions about the Bible and how to read it. This book isn't a breakdown of theology. I won't try to suggest the best way. but reading it in the context it was written in, is a good way to go about studying it. What I will say is that God gives us footprints to follow by placing people ahead of us on our journeys. He also gives us signposts to guide us if we find ourselves in a part of our journey through life where we don't have any footprints going in the direction we're heading. It has been my experience, however, that God will never leave us without some truth to guide us.

I think it's important to keep holding up the truth. I believe that God didn't cause my cancer but He definitely allowed it and this realisation was a real sticking point for me. I found it difficult to swallow that my loving God knew what I'd be going through with all the fear and pain and disability that would come with it and still let it happen. It wrecked my thinking for a while if I'm honest. But that was my reality and that's what I lived with daily with the Lord.

Throughout those early days of battle He didn't leave me, although it often felt that way. He was constantly communicating with me as long as I had ears to hear what He was saying. Even before any of this happened, God began by bringing me back to the part in the book of Acts where it says about the apostle Paul: "For I will show him how much he must suffer for the sake of my name." (Acts 9:16)

This was the first thing that God showed me through this time. I'd struggled a bit with this scripture long before my diagnosis of cancer – because it sounded like such a harsh thing to say. When it was my turn to be in that place, I had to really look at it from a new perspective. But there was something in that word about Paul that spoke, somehow, of purpose. It was for Jesus' sake that he was suffering. I know it sounds weird, but I started to think that, maybe, there's a possibility of a kind of honour in some of the suffering we go through. (Don't get me wrong, I don't think Jesus delights in domestic violence or addiction or war or sexual abuse or anything like that; it's not necessarily the thing you're being subjected to that has any benefit or merit. So many things in this fallen world are just plain evil and seem completely unnecessary and are due to selfish decisions or ignorance). I started to come round to the idea that how you go through your suffering – and how you represent Jesus in those dark times – has something special attached to it. It's in these dark and lonely times that your faith in God's Word is truly tested. Can you keep the light burning? Can you praise Him in the storm and not curse

God and die? Will you uphold the integrity of the name that saved you, or will you deny Jesus and blame Him for what's happening to you?

These are really important concepts to grapple with. It helps to have the right precepts about who God is, because then you'll understand the right concepts, so that there can be no misconceptions. Sometimes when He comes out with stuff like that, I roll my eyes, but it's true: if you hold onto the first thought that God is loving and good, then whatever comes your way must work out good in the end. The precept of loving goodness leaves no room for an ending of badness. After all, His name and reputation are really at stake. It was hard, but I came to realise that I'd been trusted to suffer for His name's sake. That's really heavy, isn't it?

There was a second thing that the Holy Spirit had whispered to me before my diagnosis, which was that they were actually going to find something in my leg.

He then gave me a word in Psalm 41:3 where it says in the NKJV (New King James Version):

> *"The LORD will strengthen him on his bed of illness;*
>
> *You will sustain him on his sickbed."*

The NLT (New Living Translation) puts it like this:

> *"The LORD nurses them when they are sick*
>
> *and restores them to health."*

I clung to that word no matter how difficult it got, even when there were times that this word was so contrary to what was going on. Don't get me wrong, there were moments I wavered as God's Word and promises seemed so far from the truth, but I took the words the Lord spoke to me as my spiritual medicine, and I chose to hold on to them and what they meant to me.

The third word I received was Psalm 46:10:

"Be still and know that I am God."

This verse had been given numerous times to both of us before the whole drama began and we didn't really know why.

The meaning in the original Hebrew text where it says, "Be still" is "raphah" which basically means to "chill out." The idea here about being still is to yield and surrender your strength and this meant that it was important for me to stay close to the Holy Spirit. Then, when my feelings would rise up within me and I would fear the worse, I would have to remember and rely on these personal words moment by moment on a daily basis. This last word was crucial as I journeyed through the whole seven years I'd been facing with surgeries and recovery. I had to stay yielded to the Lord, trusting that He knew the outcome and that it would work out well, even if it didn't seem good at the time.

My biggest question was about why it had happened. I think that if you can settle that question deep down, you position yourself to win in any situation you find yourself in. One thing I came to understand is that we live in this broken world and our bodies are in constant contact with its brokenness, so that whether you are a Christian or non-Christian, you will be negatively affected by the world's brokenness at times.

You may have sickness and difficult situations as a consequence of your environment, if not your choices. To me, the difference is made by who you go through it with. Christians understand you're not alone and the Holy Spirit will walk alongside you and keep showing you truth.

The day I was in surgery to have the original tumour removed, I bled out on the table. While this was going on, Paul was walking around the hospital praying and waiting. He told me that at one point, he sensed something bad was happening so he went into the chapel.

As he entered the ordinary-looking room, he looked on the wall and hanging on the wall was an embroidered banner with a verse on it: it said, "Be still and know that I am God." Paul said the peace of God filled that room and he knew that everything was going to be OK. This happened at the same time the surgeons were receiving skills they'd never learned and favour they didn't deserve. They stopped the bleed and I was brought back from the brink of death.

God will speak if we have ears to hear; we just need to be sensitive to hear and see Him in the midst of our darkest hour. The struggle of living in the tension of real life and faith is not easy and it's a daily choice to believe that the Lord has our best interests at heart, and that even in the most challenging situations, He cares about every detail of our lives.

When I woke up in intensive care after the operation, Paul was there beside me and I vividly remember actually tasting joy. I remember knowing I'd been in a garden with the Lord through the operation and I could taste joy. I know it sounds crazy, and I actually think Paul thought I was hallucinating from all the drugs, but it was so vivid and real for me.

This was another signpost that the Lord used to show me He was right beside me in the midst of a life-changing operation.

Through it all I felt like I was in a sort of "grace bubble." It's very difficult to describe the feeling I had through the initial stages of cancer. I had such peace and such a closeness with the Holy Spirit. It was almost like I had God's full attention and that He really cared about me, but more importantly than that, He was trusting me to carry His name in the right way. Somehow I knew that it was an important thing to do.

I'm going to share something very personal with you now: Throughout my recovery I had an angel outside of my window. This was probably the biggest sign through my whole cancer journey and you may be thinking, "She's lost the plot now," but I can truly only share what the Lord did. I was placed in my own room in the hospital while I was healing and waiting to see if the operation was a success and whether my body was going to react to the implant. I didn't know if I would ever walk again, so it was a difficult time for me. This lasted for six or seven weeks while I was attached to drips and tubes and special boots that kept my circulation steady. One crazy thing they did when I was released from ITU, which was a huge mistake, was to put me on a ward with other people who'd had knee or hip replacements. They encourage the patients to get up and moving, but for me it was impossible. One nurse kept insisting I get up and walk and I kept telling her I couldn't. Not only that but she wouldn't give me the right pain meds. It was horrible. When Paul found out he went ballistic and insisted on seeing the consultant.

As soon as the consultant found out what had happened, he went even more ballistic and that's when I was swiftly moved to my own room. I had one small window to the right of me and I couldn't move out of the bed. The hospital bed just moved up and down when you pressed the button. I had a line going into my neck straight to my heart so they could give me antibiotics and pain killers as and when needed. If I'm honest, I was in so much agony, I was taking them whenever I could.

Whenever I needed the toilet I needed to ring a bell and they would bring a bed pan and I have never felt so vulnerable and embarrassed in all my life. Sometimes it was a male nurse who came when there wasn't a women around; it was horrible. They'd lift me up and put a towel over me and wait outside the curtain until I had finished.

It was out of that little window that I became aware of the angel. I remember him being taller than the building. I say, "he" because that was what he looked like. He was carrying a sword and a shield and seemed like he was guarding the place I was in. He didn't directly look at me and I couldn't see him all the time, but I would get glimpses of him at the times I most needed courage or comfort while I was in that hospital.

There was even a time when I'd been released from my hospital bed to go to my mum's house for some respite. I think the surgical team didn't really have much hope the procedure would be successful, so they figured it wouldn't make any difference if I had a bit of time before they'd inevitably have to cut off my leg. But it was a mental lifeline to me at that moment. Paul got me situated in the car with my swollen, bandaged leg on cushions and off we went on the three hour journey to my mum's house.

Mum lives on the south coast of England, in Dorset, at a place called Christchurch. It's only a smallish house but full of character and literally a few minutes from Medford beach. She has a summer house converted as a place to live with a bathroom and cooking facilities and it was decided I'd stay in there.

Once I'd been delivered safely and settled in, Paul drove the six-hour round-trip to his mum's house in London to pick up our two children, Lilie and Tomas. You may be wondering where this is going right now, but it's an important point because my angel turned up there and stood guard outside the door. Once again, think I'm mad if you like, but one of the days my son was running in and out and I clearly remember seeing the angel actually move out of his way! I have no idea theologically how that can be explained but it was as real to me as anything else around me. God gave me an angel to guard me and he was right there with me the whole time I fought that evil cancer.

The operation was a success, as far as the original surgery to remove the tumour and insert the prosthetic implant and the false knee was concerned, but as the weeks went by my body started to reject the implant. It really felt like my body started to turn on me, and I had a continual infection. Apparently there was a "bug" on the silver-coated titanium implant and they couldn't kill it no matter how much they tried. The doctors gave me the strongest antibiotics they had but it wouldn't go. I remember feeling really unwell all the time, and I knew something was badly wrong. I was "nil by mouth" for days at a time and I was taken back into surgery to debride my leg – which is cutting away the flesh to remove the infection. After three attempts they said that if this last one didn't work, there was nothing more they can do to stop the infection.

Then once again came those terrible words: "We're going to have to amputate your leg!"

What? The operation was a success to remove the cancer but now this infection was killing me. My mind began to spin off into the dark thought that if they end up cutting off my leg, it was all for nothing.

I distinctly remember the sickly smell from my leg as it was literally rotting. The wound was yellow and green and oozing with pus. It was massively swollen and the whole length of cut was angry looking; my leg felt like an alien thing. I couldn't believe we had come this far and now this was happening.

Paul had to go home daily to pick up the kids from school and on one of those days he called me and said, "Vicky, the Lord showed me you have to speak to your leg and say you accept the prosthetic implant and receive it into your body."

At first I felt funny saying it, but I started to say the words, "I receive the implant as part of me." You might think this is a weird thing to do – maybe a bit of hysteria or pseudo-religious nonsense – but there's power in our words and up to this point I'd been praying that anything that didn't belong in my leg would be removed, not thinking that might include the prosthetic implant as well!

That same night, we both experienced something that can only be described as supernatural. I had a dream and dreamt that the wound in my leg had completely dried up and all the rot and infection was gone.

In the dream, the Lord spoke these words to me: "Vicky the enemy can only come so far. I have drawn a line. He can only come as far as I allow him. There has been a battle for your life." He showed me that the following morning the wound would be healed when they opened the bandages. Then He said to me: "You will rise again and take My message of healing to the world."

I've never forgotten these incredible words and fully believe they came from God. The first one came to pass the very morning after this experience and I hope this book will go a little way to seeing the other part of His message to me come to pass as well.

The last sign He gave me came about on the seventh year after my initial diagnosis (and the number seven biblically signifies some type of completion). I was in a prayer meeting and I saw a picture of a tomb stone with the word "CANCER" inscribed on it. I initially thought, "Oh no... is the Lord showing me that I was going to die?" The Lord told me to look closely. I thought I was going to see my name written as well and was scared to look, but it just had the word "CANCER" on it and I heard these words as the Holy Spirit whispered them to my heart: "You will never see cancer again."

I was so relieved to hear that because I was exhausted from fighting this horrible thing. My life, and my families' lives had been changed forever, and I needed some respite. You know what happened? From that day on until this point, I've not had any more surgery on my leg. My consultant openly says it's been a miracle. He insists, though, that it's a medical miracle and I'll agree that he and his team worked wonders and the technology that enabled a silver-coated titanium implant to be attached to my bones inside my leg is pretty amazing, but I know the rest of the story. It wasn't technology or human ability that dried my massive wound overnight. It was God who did that, and I'm convinced He will work alongside us or, in reality, He will allow us humans to partner with His will and plan. God puts the "super" to our "natural" and that's where amazing things take place.

I had more proof of this as the angel that I saw would keep coming back on the scene throughout those seven years and would show himself whenever the cancer needed attention. It never actually came back because it hadn't completely gone. It wasn't ever new cancer that needed surgery but it was what are known as "seeds" from the original tumour that had to be removed. Whenever there was danger, the angel was with me. It still blows my mind to this day.

He prepared me for what was ahead.

Through the seven years of fighting this cancer, these experiences and scriptures became my story. They were the basis of my reality, not the diagnosis or prognosis. Paul and I would go back to see my consultant in Oswestry or The Christie Hospital in Manchester for routine checks and bloods every three months. I can't tell you how many times we would receive news we didn't want to hear and sometimes I needed to go back in for another operation to remove more "seeds."

On those difficult days, where we even began to expect more bad news as a matter of course, when I would really struggle with anxiety, I would repeat the words that I had been given. I would speak them back to God in prayer because we wage war with the prophecy that has been spoken to us. It became a battle that I knew I'd been given the weapons to fight. It was my battle plan and God gave me signposts and the tools to fight with. But I still had to turn up and actively daily engage in the fight, with Paul always at my side agreeing with me that we wouldn't quit and would believe God for His best. I can tell you honestly that we didn't come out of those offices and hospital rooms unscathed by any means. But I did come out with my leg still attached to my body – just as God said I would.

There's one more crucial thing that happened during this time: it began to feel like life could return to some type of normality...whatever that is! God gave me a picture in prayer of a piece of land after a storm. There were branches and all kinds of debris scattered everywhere. I had the impression that this was a picture of my soul. The Lord showed me that my soul had been shredded, but the main parts were still standing, and that now He would begin the process of restoring me.

During my crisis, I'd had grace for the fight but there are always consequences to these types of battles. God deals with us according to the season we are in and it was now time to rebuild, but that's a process and isn't simply an instant waving of some kind of magic wand. I think it's important to highlight this because it's real, and some people trip up on the healing side of the journey, because they lose sight of this truth.

My experience of this restoration process was that while everyone around me was breathing a sigh of relief and looking forward to life without cancer, I felt empty and a little depressed. Maybe it was because my normal would never be the same again. Or was it was because my journey hadn't really ended – only the sickness part – and now a new battle for recovery was just beginning. One thing I knew deep down in my bones (and implant), was that God was really with me in this – that giant rock was what I clung onto with what little strength I had left.

Chapter 6

Get Out Of My Space
Protecting Your Environments

Over the years that I had cancer, my environments became crucial to my healing. Your environment means that your habitat – the place you live in as well as what you hear and what you allow in and who you allow in – must be safe enough for you to be able to concentrate on the battle you're fighting. Never lose sight of the fact that the battle is fierce and you need somewhere to be able to decompress and rest a bit.

I was going through a time where my faith was tender and delicate, and I was forming my beliefs about healing while at the same time living in a tension between faith and having a deadly tumour in my body. I realised that it can really affect you when someone comes with well-meaning words that actually leave you struggling even more than you already were.

For example, being present for a sick person is crucial, but <u>try not to say you understand what they're going through. You probably don't have a clue.</u> When people said that to me while my ruined leg was weeping pus and I couldn't walk, I'd sometimes feel like punching them. Stuff like that can seriously affect the person who is sick. Don't make the mistake of trying to liken what a sick person is going through to something you once went through because the chances are that it isn't anything like what they are going through. Sometimes, it's best to say nothing and just be there with them and for them.

There is power in the words we use every day and we rarely stop to think about that. Words can cut the soul just the same as a knife can cut the flesh. The right words can be like a surgeon cutting out a cancer but the wrong words are like a butcher chopping up a piece of meat. I understand that most people struggle to know what to say when they're confronted with sickness and pain, so my advice is to try to keep things as normal and light as possible. If a patient wants to initiate a conversation about what they're going through, by all means respond, but don't trample on them with your random medical knowledge from the internet or even from your own personal experiences. Please remember, you're not there for you, you're supposed to be there for them. Don't make the mistake of trying so hard to get your favoured position across that you ignore the position of the person on the end of your opinion.

I had a real learning experience about this when I came home after being released from hospital. I was confined to a wheelchair and I had carers coming in daily to support me. I had two young children and my husband had to concentrate on work again because, like it or not, life goes on.

One day, early on, a Christian couple that we knew from another church came to visit me. When you're stuck in a wheelchair, you have limited control of who comes in, especially when they knock at the door and your carer lets them in. After some small talk, the husband asked if they could pray for me before they left. I'm sorry for the cynicism but I could feel something about to drop and I wasn't wrong as he began immediately to pray for my repentance from sin. His motive was to get me to understand that the reason I had cancer was probably because of hidden sin in my life, and on top of that, I must have a lack of faith or else I'd be healed. To be honest, I wanted to reach across and slap him, and I'm so glad Paul wasn't there because I'm sure it wouldn't have been pretty. Please hear me when I say that I truly love God and His people, but some of them sometimes act so stupidly and weird. In my mind I was thinking, "Who is this nutter coming into my house and spouting this nonsense? Who do you think you are, coming to my house at my most vulnerable time and praying such condemning words?"

I was hurt, I was angry and was left confused and feeling very lonely. It helped a bit when I told Paul later on about what had happened and he told me that some people are just stupid. It's true! And Christians are not exempt from stupidity at times. We can all get caught up in faulty thinking.

I learnt a lot at that time about protecting your environment from certain situations and certain people. I felt my space was almost like a faith incubator and I wanted to guard it. I needed that space to be free of negativity as much as possible. The Lord was giving me an understanding of truth, and experiences with Him that I'd never previously had. It might not have made sense to some people but that didn't matter to me. They were not in my situation living through my reality.

I spoke to Paul about my need for this and we put what we thought were some necessary boundaries in place around us. This included my children because we were all going through so much stuff together. My kids now had a mum that was in a wheelchair that couldn't do all the things that she used to do. My daughter was being bullied at school at the time but didn't feel she could let us know because of what we were going through. She started losing her hair through stress – this still makes me cry more than anything. It took years for her to process what had happened enough to feel free to share this with us.

In fact, it was in 2022 when the four of us in our little family went to a conference in Los Angeles, where my now seventeen-year-old daughter had her own God experience. In a service, she was praying and asking why she'd been through so many things at the same time when she was a little girl. She told us – and a whole church that my husband was about to preach in – that God had shown her that He was preparing her for what He'd purposed for her. He said He was with her and He had always been there during those times, protecting her from the worst of it. Once again, this is hard to understand and accept if you think God should never let us face any hardship at all in life. I've come to understand that this type of utopian viewpoint can really mess people up.

When my daughter had this very real experience with God, it released something within her. She's still working through her stuff, but with a new perspective. Even my Paul, who has always done his best to guard us, came to the realisation that there are some things in life – many things – where you have to trust that God knows what's going on and that there's an ultimate plan for good wrapped up in it somehow. We live in a broken world and bad things sometimes happen because of that. You do your best to guard your environments and trust God to work everything out. It's a partnership of trust that was instituted by our Creator at the beginning of time and there's a real peace that comes when we submit ourselves to that reality.

You need practical protection.

So how do you go about protecting your environment? For me, it was about setting out some clear boundaries, expectations and ideal scenarios. Environment can be defined as a sum total of all the living and non-living elements and their effects that influence human life. In other words the circumstances, objects or conditions by which one is surrounded; it's the space you live in and it is our responsibility not to allow things into our space that are harmful or have no purpose being there.

For example, the first place I had to protect was my inner being; no one can do that for you. What I thought, spoke about and listened to was important to me, and my spiritual life became increasingly important. The time I spend daily with the Lord is the air I breath. His word at that time was like honey to my lips. He was so close to me I felt He was in the room. I actually miss Him being that close to me. He truly gets close to the broken-hearted.

I had worship music on constantly from the months I spent in a hospital bed to when I went home. I played healing scriptures and listened to teaching and preaching that I thought could help my mind. I constantly asked Paul for his perspective because of his objectivity in all of the madness I'd been subjected to. He became my medical interpreter, which was so important to me as I was working through the shock of diagnosis and life-changing surgery. I'd hear one thing emotionally from my

73

consultant and Paul would translate it to me rationally. That was so important for my recovery because it enabled me to fight the right battles and not to quit when things felt like they weren't moving quickly enough.

I came to realise that most doctors will default to giving you a worst case scenario whenever they speak to you. Paul would decipher what they were saying to me so that I didn't have to worry so much. What I heard as "mountain" Paul would tell me it was more like "molehill."

My home and my family life was an environment that I protected fiercely. We were fortunate to be able to have some adaptations done to the house we were living in at that time so I could use a toilet downstairs. We were living in a Victorian terraced house with a staircase as steep as Mount Everest and I didn't want Paul or a carer trying to carry me upstairs several times a day, so the adjustments were such a help. I also stopped allowing chaos into my home – and that really meant toxic people.

Before my diagnosis and surgery, our home was a place where the people we ministered to would come freely at all times with their problems and issues. We changed that. Having toxic people constantly come into your space isn't actually a good thing. They can leave behind some of their stuff and we realised that wasn't going to work for us in this season. So, Paul would meet with them at church or privately in a public place like a coffee shop. You can do that!

I'd still talk to people on the phone, but in the critical healing time I'd delegate others on my staff or core leadership team to work through some of the challenges instead of me doing it. Making this decision also protected our children because many people don't understand the affect being in a pastoral position can have on your kids. They see everything and if you're not careful, it can taint them. Some people break trust and mess up time and again and then blame the pastors. My kids had more than enough to deal with at this time with the challenges in our home without adding other people's problems to the mix.

All these small shifts let me focus on fighting the enemy that had tried to kill me. It's really important to have people around you who will fill you with healthy talk and direction when you're sick. Not positivity vampires who suck all the goodness out of things. Since my recovery, we've had a couple of people live with us again, but the lessons we learned then have made it so much healthier for us.

Another thing we did, because I was physically battling cancer, was to protect my physical health. I came to understand that cancer cannot exist when your body is in an alkaline state.

Scarily, much of what we put into our bodies these days is acidic. Sodas have a pH value just above stomach acid! That's mad, right? Water is key to our health because our bodies are made up of so much of it, but bottled water is mostly on the acidic side these days. It's probably been bottled for a long time before it gets to us and has been sitting in a plastic bottle since then absorbing unhealthy stuff. So we found water sources that had a high pH value. I cut out sugar, which is a bit of a cancer feeder, and even sweetener went out the window. Anything with a sugar content above five grammes per one-hundred millilitre is taking you in an unhealthy direction. Red meat was limited, which was so hard because I love a good, juicy steak. The hormones that some meat has in it are not good for you, so out it went. Dairy also went out the door. It was a battle that I was determined to win, and I mostly did all right, albeit with a few tactical retreats when my sweet tooth and steak need was too much to bear. I ate greens and vegetables, pulses and certain grains. I got out into the fresh air whenever I could and kept myself as active as possible. I broke free from the pain medication cycle as soon as I could, which wasn't easy, and in my opinion not encouraged enough by the doctors.

I don't want to bang this drum too much, but it can seem that some doctors don't really care about the very real possibility that their patients could become addicted to opiate based pain meds. I had every excuse to keep taking the opiates, but I'd been a heroin addict for goodness sake! I knew that if I didn't break that cycle, as medically legitimate as it was, I'd never recover fully. God helped me and Paul encouraged me, and by God's grace the only pain meds I take now are paracetamol- and ibuprofen-based, and only when really necessary. That, for me, is a massive protection to my environment.

Lastly, as soon as I could, I began to learn how to walk again. You don't protect your environment by being passive. I intended to get to a place where I wouldn't have to rely on other people to get me around because I'd always been so independent. So, I intentionally set out to become independently mobile as quickly as possible. It was painful and hard, but so was being confined to a wheelchair.

Because I had lost all the bones in my left leg, and with them a lot of muscle mass and nerve function, along with a drop foot and over an inch in leg length, I had to work out the best way to move. I found that I needed to gain height for the drop foot, so soles in footwear were important. Then, I couldn't push off from my foot, so I learned to lift my leg from the thigh and swing it a bit using my hip. It was really painful at first and very tiring and clumsy, but as I literally got into the swing of it, I became mobile. Make no mistake, I couldn't walk far, but it was a victory over the limitations of my environment. I was determined not to quit and with all the wardrobe adjustments we made in terms of what I could safely wear on my feet, the battle for mobility and freedom was on!

Having explained about some of the practical things we did to protect our environment, I have to end this chapter with prayer. Prayer protected our space more than anything else. I realised that God's presence and peace are the real keys to everything good that happens. He really does protect us from some of the worst of the darkness that attempts to swallow us up. His light just doesn't allow it.

When you're protected by God, there's always hope for something better to come your way. Getting into His environment has been the biggest key to my recovery. My spiritual life went deeper than ever as my devotional discipline was set. My prayers weren't so much about getting God to do things for me (although I requested a lot of things from Him at that time). It was more about being with Him. I desperately needed to be in His space.

Chapter 7

Life Changed In a Moment
Dealing with the Loss of Mobility

The last memory before my operation was having dinner at Frankie and Bennie's restaurant with my family. Everything seemed as it should be: we laughed and ate and enjoyed ourselves. The following morning, I remember saying goodbye to my two young children and Paul and I made our way to the hospital. It was my Tomas' fourth birthday.

I know that to liken loss to what I went through may seem strange but let me shed light on what I mean. On 9 July 2011, I went in for an operation as a fully active and functioning woman to remove a twenty-three centimetre tumour. The very next day, or maybe a few days later, I started to come round to the terrible understanding that I might never be able to walk properly – or even at all again. I was in extreme pain and I knew was my life was never going to be the same again. I couldn't move past that.

If I'm really honest, I'm not fully sure that I understood what the surgery meant or the massive impact it was going to have on my reality. I think I was in denial, but I started to realise very quickly that everything was going to be different. I remember seeing my leg under the bandages for the first time. Paul and Mum were there by my bedside in the Intensive Treatment Unit (ITU) and I turned my head and looked down and was disgusted at what I saw. It looked like a stranger's leg! My beautiful leg that had taken me so many places and done so many things, was a mess with massive staples holding an enormous bleeding scar running from the top of my thigh down to my foot. I couldn't stop the feeling of utter shock and loss from rising up and from deep within my being I cried, "No!" I looked at Paul then Mum and just kept saying, "No!"

As I'm writing this, tears are welling up in my eyes. I told them to please leave me. In that moment, I was alone with what had happened and I was scared and couldn't muster anything positive from anywhere.

This memory is etched into my soul. Moments like this can shake your very core and I can only reflect on how grateful I am that my identity was set and anchored upon my relationship with Jesus Christ.

I know I went into a dark place at that point. I kept asking what was the point was of all of this. How can anything good come out of this? What is it all about?

To be honest, the medication enabled me to pull an invisible duvet over my head for a few days. But I knew that unless I clawed my way back from that duvet and pain medicine demons, I might never return.

I understand why people go into a place of denial and find themselves becoming reliant on pain medication through not being able to face what life is throwing at them. A lot of my battle had to do with self-esteem and self-worth that I thought I'd surrendered to God, but I quickly began to realise how much I still had to surrender. Things I'd never really looked at before began to rise up to become real issues that I'd have to deal with. For instance, once upon a time, I'd been a long distance runner. Although I hadn't done much running in the few years previous to my diagnosis, I hated that my choice to be able to run had been taken away. I found myself getting resentful of those able bodied people who had the choice to run. I became angry about why they hadn't grabbed the opportunities in front of them while they had the chance. The truth is, you really don't know what you've got until it's taken away.

The only times I could move around during the ten weeks I was in hospital after surgery was by wheelchair. Being in a wheelchair was a strange experience. The way people treated you was understandable, but I hated it. I was still the same person, I was Vicky, but I kept feeling I was being overlooked and it seemed that people spoke over me and treated me like a victim and pitied me. It opened my eyes to how society treats disability. I felt very unattractive, not pretty and not desirable to Paul. My thoughts began to run away with things: Was he still going to fancy me? Was he going to leave me for an able bodied women? After all, we had absolutely no idea how this was all going to turn out.

These were very real feelings at that time. I felt like a burden to Paul and the kids and there were times I felt that, maybe, if I wasn't here it would be better all round. He could be freed up to marry and not be a carer to his disabled wife. I had so many feelings and so many fears in one of the darkest times in my life.

I know I've shared about the miracles and the amazing experiences we had on this journey, but there were also tough times when I was very low and didn't feel like I could continue. Honestly, I felt I wasn't a real women and wasn't able to mother my children anymore. I watched

Paul become their mother and father as he began to do all the school runs, the cooking, cleaning and grocery shopping. He even had to help me wash – basically doing everything.

When I finally returned home, there were carers to help, which was alien to me. It was uncomfortable having strangers in my house. Mum stayed with me as long as she could to help my family through this time, but even though it was such a tremendous blessing having this help, it just reinforced that I was helpless now and how crushing that realisation was.

I was on a lot of heavy opioid-based painkillers to help with the intense and constant pain. To be honest, every four hours I would look forward to numbing the pain, not just physically, but emotionally. I soon came to realise that even though I'd been told it was a necessary element of my recovery, I had become dependent on the medication. It would have been so easy to stay in that place of oblivion; I didn't want to face this life I'd been forced into. I didn't like my life at that point.

During all this, I remember the Lord spoke to me and told me to stop all the medication. I had a pain nurse at the time and she told me I couldn't do that. She said it would be madness to cut off the meds because my pain needed management so that I could cope.

Reader, I know it's impossible to understand from your perspective, but try to imagine what it is like having your leg cut open from ankle to mid-thigh, having all the bones cut away and removed and replaced with metal rods; muscle cut away and nerves removed and what's left screaming as it tried to make sense of itself. Just moving my leg sent shocks though me. The pain meds helped, but I was slowly becoming addicted to them. Don't forget, I'd been a heroin addict eleven years previously and I hated the thought of becoming a slave to drugs again. I'm not saying that anyone else should do what I did, but this was personal. I needed the pain meds for about six months after my initial surgery, but then had moved to a place where I wasn't in so much physical pain.

The truth was that things became worse for me emotionally rather than physically, so I stopped using the oxycodone. I went through cold turkey for about a week; I was shaking and not sleeping and feeling generally unwell. I was feeling messed up emotionally. I wasn't masking the real feelings anymore and it started to become really tough to face myself and my life. Paul helped me through this horrible time by constantly praying for me and encouraging me and taking the hits. Eventually he was the one who gathered up all the opioid drugs that I'd been prescribed, took them, and handed them back to the pharmacy.

I have to say that it was a scary thing for him to do, but I knew that God wanted me to take the step and trust Him. Jesus had never let me down and this wasn't my fault, so I just held on to Him as tight as I could.

The next step was challenging, but necessary and was also something to do with dependence, but in a different form. Facing the reality of this new life was tough and managing other people's perspectives of me was difficult. I needed help doing nearly everything: bathing, dressing and moving around.

I started to realise that unless I got a breakthrough internally, I was going to become disabled on the inside as well as the outside. I needed to get a freedom that had nothing to do with the limitations of my physical body. I realised I needed to get God's perspective of my situation, how He saw me and what He wanted me to do in this situation. If He wanted to use this situation for His glory, how was that going to happen? If I was going to rise again and take a message about healing to other people, then I would need to make some changes, and that could only happen inside of me.

So, I started to seek the Lord about me: who I was as this new person with a disability. I sought Him about becoming better not bitter. About becoming a fragrance not a stench. Even though I felt crushed and didn't understand the situation, I had to change the "poor me" mindset and be grateful that I still had my leg.

I started changing my thinking about the operation, too. My consultant surgeon and his team said it would not be a success, but it was a success. Not only that, I have one of the longest prosthetic implants in the world. I had the best medical care possible from one of the world's leading experts, and because of that I could still be with my children. I was also grateful that my husband had supported me and hadn't run away!

Gradually, I started to see things through a lens of gratitude, not resentment. I started to be grateful for them finding the cancer so I'd still have a future to live with my loved ones. Maybe this wasn't the end of my life, but just a blip or a bump in the road. It wasn't easy, but it was my decision and wasn't dependent on anyone else. Just like a donkey will follow a carrot, I started following my own carrot for getting better.

Chapter 8

The Carrot of My Calling
The Power of Purpose

First of all, allow me to explain what I mean about "the carrot of my calling!"

The life I lead and the things I do, along with the people I get to do it with, have all played a massive part in my healing journey. Come with me back to my hospital room in the specialised orthopaedic hospital ward:

Initially, after my first surgery, I was placed on a ward with people recovering from hip and knee replacement surgery and this threw up some challenges. As I mentioned earlier, there was a nurse who hadn't read my notes and did her best to get me up and walking immediately. That's what you have to do after having a knee or hip replaced. But most of the inside of my leg had been replaced and I wasn't supposed to put any weight on it. Also, this particular nurse refused to give me my pain medication. It all came to a head when Paul confronted her and went above her head to my own consultant.

Consequently I was quickly moved to the tumour unit where I was confronted with people in a much worse condition. Many of them had had their limbs removed, so I began to feel guilty that I still had a leg. I was so grateful to have my family support me at this key time. Mum was instrumental at that time and in my ongoing recovery. Paul was moving between our home, school and the hospital. He would pick the kids up from school and drive them to the hospital to see me almost every day whilst still pastoring and preaching at our church.

So let's get to this whole "carrot" idea. Have you ever seen the illustration of a donkey and a carrot? That donkey would follow the dangling carrot all over the place. Because it was something he wanted to eat, he wasn't going to let it out of his sight. In a similar way, my calling to serve and follow Jesus felt like a "carrot" that was forever before me. I really had experienced God's love. I'd experienced the power to change from addiction and broken dreams to being healed and fulfilled. This carrot was the knowledge that God didn't cause what happened but did have foreknowledge that I would go through this madness. So, therefore, I saw that there must be a purpose in the pain. I struggled with this at first but it gradually started to filter into my shaken mind and heart that whatever and however things happen in life, God wastes nothing. He brings purpose out of pain and a message from every mess – if we'll just trust Him.

As I read my Bible this became clearer as I read the words of Paul the apostle:

Romans 8:28 (NLT):

> *"And we know that God causes everything to work together for the good of those who love God and are called according to His purpose for them."*

My carrot also represented the fact that God could use what I was going through to transform me more and more into His image.

The Bible begins with that concept in Genesis 1:26-27:

> *"Then God said, 'Let Us make human beings in our image, to be like Us. They will reign over the fish in the sea, the birds in the sky, the livestock, all the wild animals on the earth, and the small animals that scurry along the ground.' So God created human beings in His own image. In the image of God He created them; male and female He created them."*

After my conversion, I fell in love with Jesus and wanted to grow to be more like Him. I had to stop questioning God's methods of how He accomplishes this growth in our lives. The carrot was the recognition that how I travelled through this dark valley could create footprints for others to follow.

You see, since 2003 Paul and I had been doing our best as pastors to help different people become everything that God created them to be. This work, through our church, Victory Outreach Manchester, has included all types of people including business professionals, ex-addicts and the marginalised. We've had the privilege, over the years, to see thousands of lives change by the reality of the power of God through Jesus Christ working through the ministry of Victory Outreach.

I loved doing life with these people and while I was in hospital for all those months, I can count on my hand the days that I didn't have visitors from my church, who arrived and brightened up the whole ward. These people had also experienced Jesus in the same way as me and had supported me through the whole journey. I knew that

I had a reason to live, so I kept pressing on like that cloud of witnesses in heaven. They were all cheering me on and I felt a responsibility to go through the trial both to help others in their walk with Christ, but also to give Jesus a reward for His sacrifice. I came to see that I mattered, and how I responded to this situation mattered. It was important to continue in my purpose and my calling and be there for people, even if I was in a hospital bed fighting cancer. Through those times, I enjoyed a deep sense of community and fellowship with the people that surrounded me. My hospital room was like a flower shop and I felt so much love coming from all over the world. I knew that people were praying for me. Sometimes, I could feel myself being carried through dark mind battles and negative places. I had a carrot and I wasn't going to let it go.

You may be reading this right now and feel that you are alone and you don't have a carrot. I want you to know that you're not alone. The Holy Spirit is right there waiting to reveal Himself to you. If you've never done it, simply ask Jesus to come into your heart as Saviour, Lord and friend, and let Him comfort you and grace you through whatever you're currently facing. If you've done that before but you're still in a dark place, I think having a mindset of purpose is crucial. We all need something to live for and something worth dying for. Your life matters. You matter. It also matters what you're looking at – what holds your attention in this time?

Scripture puts it like this:

Proverbs 29:18:

"Where there is no vision, the people cast off restraint;

But he that keepeth the law, happy is he."

Having vision is describing how you receive God and His ways and purpose for your life. Having spiritual revelation keeps you focused on the truth which then leads to freedom. Without it, anything goes. I've seen this happen in many people's lives when they hit some kind of crisis. I've also been tempted in my own life to use what has happened to me as an excuse not to do what I'm called to do. If you want to, you can usually justify negativity and with my cancer, I'd have a good reason to. But I felt strongly that I needed to raise a standard in my life, just as long as the Lord gave me the strength to do it. I would have a resounding "yes" in my spirit.

When we're faced with situations that are out of our control, we initially want to hold on to what we can control. We can't control anything; the only thing we can do is depend and trust on the Lord and His outcomes – the time lines are in His hands.

My calling enabled me to see a purpose in my pain. I had a choice to become bitter or better; to be a fragrance or a stench.

Although I felt crushed, I was reminded that I could be like a rose petal that is at its most fragrant when crushed. I wanted to be a fragrance of God's glory rather than the stench of my complaints.

I carried on doing ministry all the way through my sickness and disability, and continue right up to this day. I don't have cancer anymore, thank God, but I still live with a drop foot and the many challenges that have come from a life-changing operation. My hips and my back are affected and cause me pain daily. I have to make mental and spiritual choices to press forward into God's purpose. He has still called me, even though my life took a different path than I thought it would.

I want to give you an example of a time that I was nudged by the Holy Spirit to make a key choice. For the first year after surgery, Paul had been my carer and wherever I went, he was there. We are part of an international ministry, which holds various conferences and the Holy Spirit said to me: "I want you to fly to the USA to attend a conference."

Now, I had only just learnt how to walk and I was still on crutches and quite unstable, so I thought, "That's crazy!" I didn't know how my leg was going to respond to flying due to the complexity of the operation. My consultant was shocked but he said to me, "I can't stop you, Vicky. I disagree with your decision, so make sure you have good medical insurance so they can fly you home if anything happens."

That wasn't reassuring and I feel I need to explain something here as there was a deeper meaning about why the Holy Spirit had spoken to me about this. I'd become very dependent on Paul and felt vulnerable without him. There was nothing wrong with that, but it was time for something to shift in God's purpose for my life. The Lord said to me, "I am your shield and support, not Paul. I want to do something in you through this."

I told Paul what I believed God was saying to me and I told him that I felt I needed to obey God, otherwise I was going to become stuck and scared to do anything. As you can imagine, Paul was concerned. But he said, "OK, we've lived this journey of faith together and stepped out in faith where God has led us and we've seen Him come through in so many ways before: from moving to Manchester to pastoring, and from having multiple miscarriages to now having two beautiful children, so, go for it and follow where God is leading you Vicky!" It definitely helps to be married to someone that shares your faith in God.

I didn't travel alone but with someone I was close to, Jemima, who had been a new student when we met at our very first church service in Manchester (Jemima earned her PhD whilst still a member of our congregation many years later and remains a great friend to this day.).

The massive issue was that I was travelling independently for the first time in a year and I was scared. It was one of the most difficult things I'd had to do after the operation and recovery process. It wasn't just about the conference – although that gave me the reason to do it – but it was about something that needed to take place in me so I could still grow into this next season of my calling. Little did I know that what could have destroyed me, God was going to use to transform me and propel me into a season of exponential growth in our church, our lives and our calling.

I did the trip, and when I came home I felt different. There were challenges, but when I was in the USA most people I met didn't know what had happened and treated me normally. It was so refreshing, and at times I almost forgot what I'd been through. Almost, but not quite! Afterwards, on returning home, I think Paul felt a bit redundant as he took his role of caring for me very seriously and I was very grateful to him. But he was also relieved that something had broken free within me and there was light at the end of what had been a very dark tunnel.

It's amazing how breakthrough comes after you've voluntarily confronted something that terrifies you and when God is leading you to do it and you obey Him, how final that breakthrough becomes. I would never be stuck in a place of fear and immobility again. I changed because of that step of faith. I believe you can see similar things happen, too, when you follow where God leads you.

The breakthrough moment at that conference in Los Angeles in 2012 started my comeback. Today, I function better than anyone could've ever expected, including me. I made a mental decision to continue to believe that God had a purpose for me and I've come through this time with a strengthened understanding in God's faithfulness and His character. Not only that, but one year later I was asked to speak at the same conference in Los Angeles to thousands of women. As I made the long walk from backstage to pulpit, I remember feeling all sorts of emotions. So many thoughts were running through my mind:

"Will I stumble and fall?"

"Is my disabled leg really noticeable to all these able bodied women?"

"Do I have what it takes to bring a message of hope to others after everything that's happened to me?"

In spite of these thoughts and fears swirling around inside me, I had that unshakable certainty that I knew that God will never lead me into a situation to see me fail but He will allow you to overcome and become what He's created you to be. For every setback you face in life, God wants to help you make a comeback. At that conference, I was able to share my testimony of how God met me in my battle with cancer and the method He used in my situation. It was different to how I wanted things to happen, but He still healed me. The surgeons were amazing, but I truly believe they were graciously enabled to perform what one of them later described as a medical miracle. The way God healed me caused me to be transformed more into His image as I met with Him daily in my suffering.

Here's a link to that conference:

YouTube: Vicky Lloyd Women's Convention 2013

I've gone on to reach so many milestones since then and although I live every day with pain, I've learnt to continue saying yes to God at every opportunity to serve and bring Him glory. All I can really say is, I love carrots!

Chapter 9
The Impact On Others

What happened to me impacted lots of people.

Everything we go through touches those close to us in some way and they have to process things in their own way. Whilst their processing of these experiences might look different to how I'd process them, they're equally important.

I'm an individual but I play all sorts of roles in other people's lives. I'm a daughter, a wife and a mum. Wrapped up in there, somewhere, I'm a pastor's wife in a ministry which plays an important role. That ministry, Victory Outreach International, had become an extended family to us due to all the relationships we'd built over decades of doing life together.

At first, you just have to zone everything else out and survive. When you manage that, there next comes the painful stages of recovery. You can sink into a kind of "bubble" state where your focus and attention is almost selfishly fixed on things such as physical pain or mental and emotional trauma – and that's OK. In fact, it's necessary because it's our own, personal responsibility to fight those battles for the sake of our own lives. However there is a shift as you notice how dependent you are on others and you begin to see how much they've been dealing with themselves.

I came to understand that until something happens that upsets the status quo of your life, you don't realise how much we depend on the relationships we have. We take for granted things such as physical health, what we look like or our worldly status, and these get shaken to in bits. I began to see clearly how one person's sickness can affect those around them.

One scary thing I realised was that my sickness affected who I felt I was as a wife. Feeling incapable and dependant on Paul for so many things, along with feeling physically unattractive, made me feel that Paul may not want me anymore. I began to realise over the months that Paul must have faced many different issues, but he never left my side. His consistency started to show me that our relationship was made of different stuff than the superficial things we get caught up with, but I still had a daily battle in my mind.

Tough times build strong people and reveal who people are deep down. I saw Paul in a fresh light. He never complained through all those years – although he's making up for it a bit now! He still does most of the grocery shopping, which he hates, we share more of the school runs nowadays and I help out more in other areas than I used to be able to. We've found our groove and to outsiders who don't know what's happened, it probably looks like nothing has happened. I can only put thast down to the grace of God.

I've always lived by a schedule and a calendar and, if I'm honest, I got a lot of self-worth out of my ability to do things. When that was taken away, it left a gaping hole in my life and my self-worth was on the floor. I almost had to go back to the foundation of who I was without the stuff I could do. I discovered I had these deeply intimate emotions and fears and Paul saw me at my most vulnerable. It was a massive risk to allow him to see me in this place. Even the thought of him wanting to be with me with my leg amputated was horrible and having to discuss what would happen if it was removed was incredibly difficult. I'm grateful that Paul was consistent, he was by my side and became my carer.

Our sense of humour was crucial to our relationship and we would always see the funny side of things. We would laugh at ourselves and our situation a lot. In some ways, that takes the power out of it being able to hurt you. I think humour is important and laughter truly is good medicine. Studies have shown that ninety per cent of men and eight-one per cent of women report that a sense of humour is the most important quality in a partner – and it's a crucial quality for leaders. According to an article in the 'Big Think,' it's been shown to improve cancer treatments. I worry when someone has no sense of fun. Life is far too serious to be taken seriously all the time, if you get what I mean! There has to be some relief from that. In fact, something called "Relief Theory" argues that laughter and humour are ways of blowing off psychological steam. So, we laugh a lot together and I'm grateful that Paul made his choice to stay by my side.

We say vows when we marry and that includes the sentiment of committing to our spouse "in sickness and in health." I'm honestly not sure we really know what that means. When you're young and healthy it's difficult to imagine anything else, but it's the reality for many marriages that sickness comes and unless the partnership is built on something deeper than superficial things, it probably won't stand the tests that will come. We both had to come to a place where we trusted one another to be truly honest about our fears and the realities of what was happening.

I was a mum of two young children who needed me and I wasn't able to run after them everywhere anymore or to go to soft-plays or to carry them or to pick them up when they fell. I was stuck in a wheelchair or on crutches and it left me feeling powerless and unable to be the mum they needed. They naturally gravitated to their dad, who had become their caregiver and this hurt me at the time – it hurt a lot! I think Tomas wasn't aware, as he was too young, but I know my Lilie was aware and wasn't able to express her true fear of losing me.

I remember that one time I was able to collect the kids from school. I was so excited and was going to go to the playground and wait for them both. When they came out, Lilie went to Paul and seemed distant to me. Tomas just jumped on me because he was just glad to see his mum, but Lilie was a little older and was seemingly more aware of what others thought and was a bit embarrassed. Initially, I was upset and angry and wondered if she realised what it took to walk round on crutches. It took a lot, but I came to realise it didn't matter because in her little world, she didn't want anything to be different. I needed to accept that she wasn't going to understand things from my perspective because she was just too young.

We did our best to guard how much we told Lilie and Tomas about my cancer and all the treatment I had over the following six-plus years; but my daughter still struggles to speak about what she went through in her innocent little mind. Even now when we talk amongst ourselves about the cancer, she becomes very emotional and still worries about it coming back, along with the possibility of losing me. I can reassure her, but I can't promise her it won't happen, although I do truly believe I'm done with that phase of my life. The tough reality is that Lilie grew up in a family that lived with the knowledge that I was fighting a battle with something that was doing its best to kill me.

As a family, we adjusted to a new way of life with me having a drop foot, a mangled leg and a disability. We had the house adapted with a toilet downstairs and grab-rails around which enabled my home to become my safe place. If we went anywhere outside, Paul would make sure the ground was level with no steps and no cobbles so I could manoeuvre without too much trouble.

Tomas and Lilie were aware that daddy had to also take care of mummy and not just them. Something beautiful happened in our family as our kids became more resilient and caring. That quality in our relationship is still in place today. Paul's role changed, never to return to how it was and that is how life works. In all this, though, he built a closer relationship with the kids that is still in place today and I'm truly grateful for many of the things that came out of that time. We're closer for it, but I can understand how sickness can cause major challenges in relationships as there are many crossroads. Unless a common ground is found families can very easily fall apart.

My advice is to keep talking to each other. Do your best to be real with your feelings – even if that fear seems stupid! If you're ever in a mad situation like this in your life, which if we're honest is likely at some stage to some degree, you're going to have lots of crazy thoughts pinging about in your mind. The way to tame them is to get them out of your mind and give them shape by giving them words that can be captured and brought into a place of order and reality. And, hopefully, obedience to who God is and what He can do. Never forget: you don't have to be on your own through this process and shaping your personal thinking in this way can be literally lifesaving. Talk about everything you can with other, safe people concerning what you're going through. Don't let negative thoughts squat in your mind but get what help you can to evict them. The fact is you'll never be able to live a positive life with a negative mindset. This will not just benefit you, but also all the other people in your life who are affected in some way by what has happened. People can't help you with what you don't share, and you'll be surprised how much help there is available.

Another thing that I believe helped my recovery was eventually being able to step outside my own little bubble and listen to, and attempt to understand, the impact on those closest to me. In sickness scenarios, it's usually the patient who gets all the attention, but what happens to the others? What are they going through? How do they manage their emotions and what do they do to cope? I think this is so important because your healing is often secured by how they adapt and overcome all the challenges they face. Be sure to give them a voice as well because without those loved ones, you'd be swimming alone in that sea of misery. I want to give you a glimpse of what happens to the others in your life with some questions I asked Lilie and Paul:

What happened to your world as mine was collapsing?

How did you feel?

How did you cope?

I hope this helps you and gives some insight into what else is happening in your orbit. And I pray it will give you permission to be heard and not to worry that you're betraying your role or falling short in your duty. When we can fight as one, we're so much stronger.

Here are Lilie's and Paul's thoughts:

Lilie's Journey

I don't really remember when I found out the news about my mum having cancer and I certainly don't remember knowing the impact it would have on my life. This chapter has been very hard to write as, to this day, I still deal with the fear of cancer and the pain of almost losing my best friend in the world. But I know by writing this I could possibly help someone who has gone through something similar. So for that reason, I'm ready to conquer my fear.

This is my side of the story...

At the time we found out the news, I was just a child, but old enough to feel the pain of a sick mum. Me and my mum share a similar feeling when one of us is sick or in pain in whatever way – the other one can feel it. This is the only way I can explain how I feel when I talk about her cancer and how I felt in that time; I would rather have been in that position than my mum. I seemed to have blocked most of this period in my life out of my memory, but my mum told me that clumps of my hair used to fall out. I think this was because I felt like I was going through the cancer alongside my mum. But also, I'm ashamed to say, as a little girl with all the self-conscious feelings that you feel when you're growing into yourself, I thought a lot about me instead of my mum and dad.

My dad was like a superhero. He would wake up, take me and Tom to school, then drive to Wales to see my mum, drive back to pick me and Tom up, take us to the hospital in Wales, and then take us all home at night. He'd do that every day. Even without barely any money at the time, he had faith that there was a way every time. But this was really hard for me. My mum and dad were preoccupied, but not by choice. This is why I felt alone at a time where I was also getting bullied for my weight by the boys at school. I felt I had no one to go to – not because they didn't care but because, at this point, I felt there was much bigger things to focus on. This led me to be angry and depressed at a young age. I would always blame God for giving cancer to my mum: "Why does this have to happen to me?" "Why are You taking my mum away?" And still years later, I continued to ask why.

Paul's Journey

I'm a strange person. When things get crazy and people around me start panicking, everything for me seems to get slower and clearer. It's almost as if I'm at my best when everything around me is falling apart. If I'm honest, I get a bit worried about that, but that day, when we heard Vicky's cancer diagnosis, my weird ability became a real blessing.

Thinking back, I can remember my heart lurching and a coldness in my belly, but then my mind started whirring into battle mode. The only way I can describe it is that my mind started running all sorts of calculations about the situation. There were things happening beyond my control that were put on a shelf somewhere inside my mind, and I was left with what I could realistically do. I knew I had to somehow find out God's mind regarding this situation, so I immediately began to fast and pray – and I mean really pray! Then, something wonderful happened to me: an overwhelming sense of peace came upon me and the reality of peace stayed with me for the whole seven years that Vicky fought so hard to overcome that wicked cancer. I know I fundamentally changed as a man during that period, but I can only say that it was God's doing rather than mine.

The first thing I did was try to reassure Vicky. She was in shock at first and later on went into a place of denial but, to her credit, she kept facing the right direction, gritted her teeth and kept moving forward. I saw her bravery first hand and it awed me. If I'm honest, I did all the, "I wish it was me instead," stuff but I doubt I'd have handled things half as well as she did.

The first thing I really had to face was about our future together. Would I have to become Vicky's carer forever? What about our family and our dreams and plans? What about our ministry that was taking shape after years of sacrifices and challenges? Would we lose everything? What would all this mean for me? I admit I had these thoughts, and I think they're normal. My decision wasn't hard to make, really. I love my wife and I made what I believe were solemn and holy vows before God and witnesses that I'd pretty much love her through thick and thin, for richer or poorer and in sickness as well as in health. So, it was a no-brainer. I'm a man of duty – it's how I was raised by my father and how I was trained by the ministry of Victory Outreach; so that was that, job done. I'm staying for the whole ride.

The next thing to look at was a bit trickier. What did God want to happen in this situation? Fortunately, He gave me pretty clear instructions, which has already been detailed elsewhere, but I have to admit there was immense pressure when I was delivering that instruction to the medical professionals. If I was wrong, I could be responsible for my wife's death. All I can say is that I had that supernatural peace enabling me to push for something that wasn't even originally on the cards. The proof that it was God leading those decisions, is the miraculous outcome we've seen take place. I'm so glad we went down that route. It's been incredibly difficult and Vicky has shown an amazing amount of bravery and determination, but the result is that she still has her leg, albeit a bionic one. What a result!

All this was pure grace, really, added to my peculiarly unemotional personality. It hasn't been easy, but it seemed pretty simple at the time and I'm just trying to make the point that whatever good things happened, I can't take any credit.

There were also many things to take on the chin as the journey to healing progressed. For example, doctors treat you like you're invisible when you're not their patient. That was true for me, at least in the beginning.

I quickly learned how to get seen, though. Don't forget, the patient is often in a state of shock and they need someone as a kind of bodyguard to protect them from making bad decisions. I also found myself interpreting what the doctors were saying as I could listen without any filters of pain or fear. I made sure I was at every appointment and I was with Vicky at hospital everyday bar one or two. That daily journey took its toll due to the constant trips and the added worry of expense. Add to that our two really young kids and I had some real life adjustments to make.

To say I changed because of this doesn't really do justice to what happened inside of me. I had to become a mum as well as a dad, at least for the first few years of surgery and recovery and then more surgery. Between Vicky, the kid's schooling and the house and pastoring a growing church, I had no time for myself. Strangely, it was my physical health and not my mental health that suffered the most. I snatched meals and slept badly, literally for years. But through all that, I became stronger on the inside. I became very resilient and learned the tough lessons of self-adjustment and adaptation. These lessons have been invaluable as time has gone by. Would it surprise you if I told you I've had much rougher times than this personally in later years? One thing I know is that God allows things to happen in one season that will prepare you for other tough seasons in life. Every time Vicky was due for a check-up at the hospital – every three months – it would be hard a day before and a day or two afterwards, and we'd have to gear ourselves up for possible bad news.

I knew God was with us, but I had a constant, underlying hum of anxiety that tried to get me to believe that I wouldn't be good enough to cope with everything. I still have that! It's a real tension sometimes. One of those places of concern was the church we pastor. I felt torn between all these responsibilities and I didn't want the church to suffer. We'd worked with so many people and I had to scale back on that a bit because Vicky needed me. I remember one day praying and basically asking God to take care of the church so I could take care of Vicky. I didn't want to let anyone down, especially God. I'm aware that there's a lot of theology involved with this and maybe I shouldn't have been thinking like that, but I had to work all this out in a pressure cooker.

What made coping so much easier was the bravery that Vicky showed every day. Her determination and faith got stronger as she literally battled for her life. Sure, there were days when things looked dark and stress and fear tried to overwhelm her, but she didn't bow to a negative outlook. All I did was make sure she had the information she needed and the environment to heal in. The heavy work was something she did. She amazed me, and she still does. She's a champion.

We lived on the very edge for seven years as we went for three-monthly check-ups, receiving bad news more than once about more surgery needed. Our church was growing, which is a great thing to happen, but adds more pressure as more people demand your time and energy, and our little children were growing bigger and their needs were changing. Our daughter was having some challenges at school and our son had severe asthma, which meant that as he's adventurous, there were injuries and hospital visits for his breathing problems, plus his cuts and scrapes. It was a full-on life and we just did our best to live it. We loved and served others and preached what we did our best to live.

I found that there's a strange reality about living on this strip of life between madness and blessing, which is similar to riding a bike. If you move too slowly, you'll struggle to stay upright, whereas if you achieve and keep good momentum, it becomes easier to travel where you want to go. That's all we did. We just didn't slow down too much or quit. The result was a momentum that caused us to blow through many of the challenges we faced.

One last thing that kept me going were the people around us. Community is key. My parents, Des and Pat, were incredibly supportive, and Vicky's mum, Dorrie, was always there to help when needed. A lot of our church friends didn't really understand what we'd been going through – because the reality is that everyone gets on with their own lives – but we had enough support from some really special people that lifted us when we were just about holding our heads above the waves.

Our children are champions as well. It took a lot for them to be as balanced as they are now and their resilience and strength of character is a beautiful thing to see as a father. We're a tight knit family, because I believe that's how it should ideally be and I'm all in for them.

I'll leave this little snapshot with two things:

Firstly, the day we spoke to Vicky's surgeon, who's a professor now, and he gave her the all-clear with the words, "It's a miracle!" – that was a special day. It was special, even though he still clings to the thinking that it was a medical miracle and not a God-inspired one. It became more special when he started saying that he didn't know where the skills came from as he performed the original surgery and how everything went in favour of the procedure and how it's in the record books as the longest prosthetic implant they'd ever done.

I reminded him of the words God gave me all those years previously: "You'll get skills you've never learned, you'll have favour you don't deserve and this will be the one they'll write you up for in the record books." He remembered it well and just shook his head and agreed that it had been a miracle.

The second thing is that today Vicky lives her life with a massive disability that no one would realise, unless they were told. She's like a bionic woman, because what tried to kill her has enhanced her abilities in so many ways. She is such an overcomer and she loves and leads and inspires people all over the world. We've faced many challenges since then and life continually needs to be faced, but I know that God is with us and really all the credit goes to Him.

Chapter 10
Fighting the Unseen Battle
The Spirituality of Sickness

There are many battles that we'll fight as we journey through life. Many of them will be fought in the natural arena and involve everything from upbringing and education, through health and finances and relationships, to loss and death and broken dreams. These natural battles have enemies that you can often see and even touch; frustratingly, some are just out of range.

I was raised in a family that used confrontation as a way to resolve almost everything, so I feel better with enemies I can see. My diagnosis was something like that; at least in the beginning. The physical aspect of it was something I could see and feel and that gave me a target to fight against. The facts were that I had a very large tumour that was life-threatening and unless God healed me by removing it, and unless we made a decision to do something with it, I would eventually be killed by it. These natural battles are never easy, but at least they're simple.

But there's also a spiritual battle that we need to fight, with an enemy that comes to steal, kill and destroy. I knew deep down that this infirmity wasn't from God. Jesus promises to give you life and life in abundance and every good gift is from the Father in heaven. I'd read these things in the Bible many times and to my thinking, I believed it. But there was a tension in my situation that I really struggled with.

For a long time, I couldn't reconcile the fact that God knows all things and He knows the beginning from the end and, therefore, He knew that I was going to get sick – and still He just let it happen! For some reason that was like a body blow to my understanding of theology. Paul kept telling me that God hadn't caused it but He'd allowed it, which is almost as bad because, for a while, I just couldn't get my head around that concept.

God is all powerful and all knowing, but this slipped through the net, somehow. What was going on there? Why do bad things happen to Christians if God is such a good God? This has got to be the number one question we are asked as ministers and here I was right in the middle of the confusing reality of it. I had to wrestle with these thoughts and come to a personal place of conviction about what I believed because the spiritual battle I needed to fight started becoming real.

We had already had Paul's experience with a demonic spirit in our house and I'd had an angel guarding me. I quickly realised that the battle for my life wasn't just a natural, physical one but also a spiritual one.

The only thing I knew to do was to pray and begin studying Scripture to get a revelation of what God wanted me to do. In prayer, some things began to make more sense to me. This became important because there were many times I felt like I was sinking into the diagnosis and it would have been easier to pretend it wasn't happening. I came to realise how subtle the spiritual forces of darkness are and how they use negative suggestions with the aim of getting you to personalise and internalise them. If that happens, they've caught you in their trap and you'll find yourself turning into a shell of who you're supposed to be. I knew no one else could fight this battle for me. If I didn't get up and fight for my life, I'd become a victim of my circumstances. I realised that everything around me depended on whether I was going to allow or not allow this evil thing to defeat me.

I also began to truly understand the consequences of living in a fallen world. That's biblical terminology for the fact that our environment and our society is messed up: from wars and diseases to greed, lust and corruption – it's not how God originally created it to be.

Everywhere on this planet, there are man-made problems and disasters that could be avoided if greed and pride and selfishness wasn't so common. These can impact our lives in many ways. As believers, we're told we have this body and that it's a temple that carries the Holy Spirit, which promises us huge benefits. But our bodies constantly come in contact with this fallen world and we can get sick from it. There are contaminants and viruses and poisons and toxins that can attack our health, and much of it is caused by humanity's inability to follow God's instructions on how to live.

Our minds are bombarded with opinions and ideologies that attempt to turn our attention away from God and people will automatically blame Him for everything that goes bad. They're not so quick to thank Him when things go well! That's what a fallen world looks like and it takes its toll on our overall health: mentally, emotionally, physically and by no means least – spiritually.

We're born into this world as natural men and women and when we become born-again, we become new creations and all things are new. But what becomes born-again is the spirit within us, not our bodies. That comes at another time at the resurrection and until then, our bodies are subject to the same fallen environments as everyone else in the world. Unfortunately, this means that trouble can still come to us all, even if we're Christians.

The realisation, that the world is sick and I'm in the world so I can get sick, was something that was crucial to my ability to fight the spiritual battles I was facing. Then came the conviction that the difference is that the Lord promised He will be with us and that we're to take heart, or courage, that Jesus has overcome the world.

There are so many scriptures and examples in the Bible that speak into this stuff and as I immersed myself in them, my mindset and attitude changed. It took time but it strengthened me and it's amazing how vital your thinking is. Everything starts in the mind: from your initial thoughts comes a physical response and whether we like it or understand it fully or not, where your thoughts lead, your body will follow. This is not just about positive thinking but the truth is you'll never live a positive life with negative thinking.

There are scientific studies that show the link between our thinking and the physical response to that – so I'm not over-spiritualising this point. Hormones are released from the actions of our minds that lead to responses in our bodies, from stress to problems about how we function. It's a real thing.

Another truth that became foundational in my journey towards healing is about my true identity, or the understanding of who I belong to. This gives us a real starting point to work from. I'm a child of God and I'm adopted into His family and this identity has implications for how I'm supposed to live. It became apparent that I had to become reconciled to the fact that if I belong to God, He will heal me the way He chooses to do so, not necessarily in the way I'd choose it to be done. This was a big thing for me. It settled the idea that I might never be healed fully in this life, but it didn't matter because one day, I'll be made new and be completely whole again – because that's God's promise. It might sound strange, but these things armoured my mind. I started to become almost bulletproof from the subtle and sometimes not-so-subtle attacks from our spiritual enemy.

I've also found that our five senses become more real in times of crisis than our spiritual senses – but that's where prayer and the Word of God play such a crucial role in the healing process. Why? Because the Truth contained in Scripture moves through those senses to a deeper place of reality. Those natural senses of sound and sight and taste and smell and touch can be used in such a negative way against us. The sound of a doctor saying the words again and again that, "Cancer has come back," and the sights and smells of a hospital ward, or the feeling of constant, nagging pain plus the nasty taste of hospital food (I'm joking – not!), meant that I needed other words to counteract the negativity. That's when I had to go back to my secret place with the Lord and ask Him what to do. I'd ask, "What do you say about this?" And He'd whisper back to me, or confirm, what He'd said before. Words such as:

The LORD sustains him on his sickbed;

in his illness You restore him to full health.

Psalms 41:3

Be still and know that I am God.

I will be exalted among the nations,

I will be exalted in the earth!

Psalms 46:10

But when Jesus heard it He said, "This illness does not lead to death. It is for the glory of God, so that the Son of God may be glorified through it."

John 11:4

One key word I sensed God give me one day in prayer was this: "I've drawn a line for your life. The enemy can only come so far. There has been a battle for your life but you'll rise again and take My word of healing to the church and the world."

You may not believe that God speaks to us like this, but I can't deny what it did to my faith and my healing process. God would whisper to me that He wanted to shine His glory through my life. Also things such as: in my weakness His power is being made perfect; and although the enemy was buffeting me, His grace was sufficient for me.

There are so many scriptures that God used and still uses today that comfort me. There will come an end to cancer. Sometimes, His presence was so tangible and His voice so clear that even though it often felt like my body was wasting away outwardly, inwardly I was being renewed day by day.

If I didn't stay aware of the spiritual battle daily, it would've crushed me. But through His grace and daily bread and the words He whispered to me, I was able to fight the battle. God taught me to fight regardless of my physical disability by teaching me that I was free on the inside, regardless of what was happening on the outside.

If I'm honest, the transformation that happened inside of me couldn't have happened unless I'd gone through the years of sickness. I'm grateful for the journey I've been on as it has forged and formed me more and more into the image of Christ. It's a choice to respond to God in the situation you find yourself in, whatever that may be, but choosing God's way is always the best way.

I had countless miracles through this healing journey and as I've mentioned previously, I had an angel to war for me.

It's the personal touches that have stayed with me most, however, such as wanting to share some time when I had been released from the hospital to go to Mum's for respite with my two kids, who were four and six years old at the time.

We were staying in her summer house in the garden and I remember it was a beautiful day. I was on the bed and the kids were playing on and off the bed, as they do. I wasn't feeling well and later that day, I would be taken back to the hospital as I had another infection, but the kids kept running out of the summer house door. All of a sudden, I became very aware of the angel by the door. I saw him. What blew me away was the fact that he opened the door to let the kids in and shut it again. I know what you're thinking. But this spiritual being was guarding the door and it amazed me because it felt so personal. He was letting my kids in and out as I lay there feeling useless. It really touched me. I'm fully aware some people are sceptical of these things happening, but I'm standing by my experiences. My husband is deeply theological in what he believes and he agrees – although he does complain that I get the angels and he only gets the demons.

Learning to walk again, with no muscles, sinews or nerves in my left leg and with a false knee and no feeling in many places, meant learning to walk in a different way. I had to walk entirely from my thigh, not being able to rely on my foot or lower leg. It was a long and painful process. I felt like giving up so many times. I remember being told on four occasions that the cancer was growing again and I would need to have more operations. The battle in my mind was so real, but setbacks don't have to define you. You can choose how you think. That's what repentance is all about: taking your thoughts captive and making them obedient to Christ. Paul calls this "the master key" of transformation and it's all about a decision that comes from our minds.

My mind was the greatest battle of all and I truly believe our minds are powerful and hold the key to our healing. We all have choices when setbacks happen and I decided that they would be milestones on my journey of healing and not millstones around my neck, trying their best to drag me down to destruction. I became more and more certain that there was life after my diagnosis, even though I'd thought that before. I really know, now, that even though the battle for the mind is a difficult one, when you fix your mind on Jesus and what's He's done and make decisions based on what He says, the odds are in your favour. With God in your corner, every setback has the possibility of seeing you make a comeback and win a victory over your enemies and your challenges. So don't stop fighting.

Epilogue
Where I Am Now

I've been trying to write this book for three years and I've struggled to do it – for several reasons. The first one is that it brought up so many emotions attached to all the memories of everything I went through. I didn't realise that I'd stuffed so much down until I tried to remember it.

I think the biggest feeling or fear that came up was the lack of control and that anything could happen – and maybe it would happen again! I found myself becoming worried and a bit fearful and decided to put it down. However that gentle still, small voice whispered, "I want you to write this book because the journey of healing is important for others to hear."

I've definitely said to myself and others that I'm not a writer; I don't have the time; I don't think anyone would want to read about my journey. There have been many different voices crowding in on my mind trying to stop me putting all these memories and facts together. But here I am, writing the epilogue; nearly finished!

All I can think is that it's my story and I've written it in the best way I can. I do believe it will bring hope and faith with guiding steps that can help people through difficult seasons, so they can come through with their faith intact. The journey may not look like they thought it would and probably won't unfold how they thought it would, but with the right attitude and perspective towards the Lord, then good can be brought out of it.

Who am I?

This is a question that's become more settled for me. I shared in this book, in the early chapters, about my upbringing and how this affected me in so many ways: my identity; my self-esteem; my mind; my whole person was shaken by what happened between my parents and the transactional, conditional love which shaped my understanding of relationships.

Today, I'm a lot more secure in who I am in Christ. I think the long season of sickness and the daily wrestle with my faith has brought me to a place where I'm not moved by much at all. My character was formed through the trials I faced because what I believed and who I believed in was truly tested. It feels like my roots have gone down deeper through what I went through and now my identity in Christ has been made stronger and is established on much firmer ground.

My Calling

My calling to minister also changed during this time and became stronger and more urgent. Many of the distractions that life throws up, along with the temptation to live a mostly self-centred life, became less important and seductive than before I became sick. Perspective is a huge thing to manage because it's the lens we view our lives through and mine got clearer and more focused on the reason I was alive.

I've always known I was called to work with women from all backgrounds and to disciple them to become all they were created to be, but this calling went deeper into my very bones. I have always known I was called to support Paul in whatever capacity he needs me as well, but I realised there was a calling for me to speak, teach and lead in my own right. It wasn't something I had to strive for, it became who I was. Doors began to open for me to speak and lead on different levels, firstly in Victory Outreach International and then also across the UK and beyond. I don't think I need the carrot anymore because I've truly morphed into the woman Christ wanted me to be. I'm still working out that journey and what that looks like in the next season. I recognise that if I had allowed the trial to stop me from growing, I would not be where I am today. I'm still on the potter's wheel, but I'm moving in the right direction.

Health

Since 2017 – when I received the picture of the tombstone with the word "CANCER" on it and when the Lord whispered to me, "You'll never see cancer again" – this has literally become my truth. I have yearly scans on my leg and lungs for any reoccurrences. However, today, I am cancer free.

I have daily struggles with my mobility, but I stretch myself daily by walking as much as I can with Ronnie, my dog. Daily, I face pain and regularly, my leg just seems to give way and I find myself on the floor. This has caused me, at times, to feel very vulnerable and I have to push myself not to just hide behind the pain and disability even though it's the reality of what I deal with.

I know there isn't much I can't face with God and I choose not to take pain meds unless I am bedridden. If that happens, I manage the pain and after three days, maximum, I stop and will only use non-addictive pain meds. I refuse to hide behind having Paul as my carer, or any another excuse based on my circumstances.

When I fly it can be a real struggle as my leg swells and I struggle to walk afterwards. But, again, I force myself and the swelling goes down, eventually. I have thoughts of the future and what it holds with my health, not so much cancer but the size of the operation and if anything will need to be replaced. I can't go there, though. I would like to say I have all the faith to be OK with it but it scares me. I don't want to be opened up again and go through the operations and the process of walking and rehab, and I also don't want my family to have to go through all that again. I leave all that in God's hands and trust Him that He'll take care of it. He has done it up to this point and proven to us how faithful He is. There's no point worrying too much about the future because that robs today of its joy – and there's a lot to find joy in our lives when we look properly.

What I'm Doing Now

Today finds me pastoring alongside my husband and our beautiful, crazy Church Victory Outreach Manchester. It's full of people from all walks of life. We reach out to drug addicts and prostitutes who become part of our community alongside doctors, dentists and students. We have single people and families and serve forty different nationalities. We worship the Lord together, growing together in Christ as we journey through the ups and downs of life. My husband and I also have the privilege to oversee other churches in Scotland, England and Germany, and we soon hope to plant a church in Ireland. I've had the privilege to speak all over the world in many different places and I love it. My life is full of purpose and I feel like I'm living out my mission and nothing tops that.

My Family Now

A lot has happened throughout the years as I battled cancer and I think it forged us together. We're very close now. We do most things with each other and whenever we can, we travel with our children and do our best to include them in our experiences.

I don't think it's easy being pastor's kids, with the transitions and changes that happen in churches, but I believe it has made them stronger. We talk, we laugh, we cry and give each other space to go through the ups and downs of life.

Lilie shared earlier about the impact my cancer had on her and how she had such a difficult time processing the questions about why a good God would allow her mum to go through all that. She was very bitter and angry for many years, even blaming God. The fact is, children perceive what they perceive and have to grow in their understanding that just because you're a Christian, it doesn't mean that bad things won't happen, but God gives us the strength to get through. Lilie has had some beautiful experiences with the Lord in the last year as God is beginning to heal her and speak to her about her future and the purpose for the pain she's been through. It's been a journey with her faith but I know the Lord has my children in His heart. He's given me promises for them and He's faithful.

As I write this book, I'm now a parent to two teenagers and I love being a mum. Although the ups and downs of preparations for exams come with many challenges, they are great kids. They both attend our church, which does bring me joy, and although it's been a mad journey, God has His way of drawing them to Him.

My Future Now

I don't know what the future holds but I do know the One who holds the future. I want to finish this book and then look at writing a testimonial book for other people caught in addiction and crime cycles. I want to be able to send it into women's prisons, because that's where I first got touched by the Holy Spirit. I read the book 'Run Baby Run' by Nicky Cruz in my cell and I felt hope for the first time that if God can change his life, there's hope for me. I'm grateful that I've been able to meet Nicky personally and my husband has helped in his missions in different countries. Nicky even came to preach at our church in Manchester, where we saw many people came to Christ. Isn't it amazing how God works out His plans for us?

I have a message of healing that the Lord has given me through all that I've been through: that even though He doesn't always heal in the way we think He will, He always heals. Whether that be through doctors, medicine or in heaven, He wins.

I truly hope this journey I went on – through cancer with all the ups and downs – helps you in your situation. It's the ups and downs that are the making of our crowns, so straighten yours. And when life throws a curve ball at you, throw it straight back and start to learn to juggle this new season with the wisdom and understanding and daily leading of the Holy Spirit.

About the Author

Vicky Lloyd is from Bournemouth and comes from a broken family. At a young age, her life spiralled into a ten-year journey of drugs, addiction and crime until she was introduced to Jesus by a nurse as she lay in a hospital bed.

By God's mercy and grace, as a wife, mother and pastor, Vicky today stands in total freedom, drug-free and healed of bone cancer and hepatitis. Vicky and her husband, Paul, are senior pastors of Victory Outreach Manchester and regional overseers of seven churches. Vicky is also involved in the teaching program for the residents in the Victory Outreach Homes.

Facebook: Victoria Anne Lloyd

Instagram: @victoria_lloyd_vomcr

Email: leadingbrokenwomen@gmail.com

Website: https://www.leadingbrokenpeople.com/services-9

CANCER VS THE **BIONIC ME**

Printed in Great Britain
by Amazon